HOW TO LIVE WITH
YOUR TEEN-AGER

Books by Dorothy W. Baruch

HOW TO LIVE WITH YOUR TEEN-AGER

ONE LITTLE BOY

NEW WAYS IN DISCIPLINE

GLASS HOUSE OF PREJUDICE

YOU'RE OUT OF THE SERVICE NOW *

PARENTS CAN BE PEOPLE

YOU, YOUR CHILDREN AND WAR

PERSONAL PROBLEMS OF EVERYDAY LIFE *

PARENTS AND CHILDREN GO TO SCHOOL

* With Lee Travis

How to Live with Your Teen-Ager

BY DR. DOROTHY W. BARUCH

ILLUSTRATIONS BY LOIS FISHER

NEW YORK   TORONTO   LONDON

McGRAW-HILL BOOK COMPANY, INC.

HOW TO LIVE WITH YOUR TEEN-AGER

Library of Congress Catalog Card Number: 53-8015

FIFTH PRINTING

Published by the McGraw-Hill Book Company, Inc.
Printed in the United States of America

TO MY MOTHER

whose ever-young spirit
makes seventy
still enjoy seventeen

A Few People I Would Especially Like to Thank

A multitude of people have studied the adolescent. They have measured his bones. They have assayed his intelligence. They have listened to his speech, observed his actions. They have looked with perceptiveness and vision into his fantasies and his dreams. They have watched him struggle through and come to grips with the ebb and flow of the cultural life that surrounds him. They have compared him as a sophisticate with his more primitive brother. Out of the meeting and mingling of various disciplines, the light comes reflected from many facets. I am grateful if I have been able to catch some of its rays on these pages.

More intimately and closely am I grateful to a small group of former students—now public-school teachers and good friends—who contributed some of the examples of what boys and girls in high school and junior high school have thought and said and done. My thanks in this regard go particularly to Alice Bohem, Paul Bohem, Dorothy Johnson, and Boyd Mathews.

My thanks go also to Judy Wolf who helped to think up the picture ideas, and to Lois Fisher who executed them so delightfully.

I am grateful to those parents and teen-agers who shared their thoughts and feelings with me and gave me whatever aliveness these pages achieve.

I am grateful, too, to Lenore Gillies who, in spite of full days, managed to decipher and put into shape my first rough draft; and to Carol Moss who, with friendly zeal, retyped the many revisions and with intelligent skill brought into shape the final copy.

And once more I am most grateful of all to Hyman Miller, my husband, who, out of the rich background of his knowledge, checked the validity of the medical and psychosomatic material, and who, out of the rich generosity of his spirit, constantly gave criticism and encouragement, fortifying me warmly in the struggle that invariably comes with giving birth to a book.

Contents

[ix]

Part Two

THEY CRAVE A NEW DEAL IN SEX EDUCATION

[x]

[xii]

PART ONE: TOWARD

BETTER UNDERSTANDING

1. You Needn't Be at Cross-Purposes

No time in the life of parents brings as many puzzling questions as does that period when their children are in the teen years. At no time are parents as apt to feel so perplexed and so much in need of new understandings.

You look at your daughter with the woman's curves beginning to shape her body, and for a fleeting moment you see in her the baby whose curling fingers clung to your hand some twelve years earlier. You look at your son reaching for his razor, and for a second you see the stocky little boy who took his first wobbly steps across the carpet some thirteen years back. They are the same people, yes. They have the same bodies grown bigger. The same minds. But a bewildering change has come over them. They are no longer little children. Neither are they men or women. And yet we who are their parents feel the same responsibilities for them. We still need to manage, guide and help them. Legally, morally, spiritually, this is our desire and goal.

Because the task of helping children through the teen years is such a vital one, we are searching as we have never searched before for courage, wisdom and deepened insights.

Fortunately today there are things to know that can lessen

old misconceptions which have stood between us and our children. There are things to learn that can make us better able to help them grow into the kind of men and women we want them to be and who are so urgently needed in today's world. Out of these can grow new understanding and new faith in ourselves.

WHAT PARENTS FEAR

Ever since the bursting of the fearful bomb in Hiroshima, we have known that our children are facing an age different from any previous age. They will have to possess the courage and the ability to stand up for what they feel is right; the ability to defend it. They will need to be strong where strength is called for and gentle where gentleness can help. They will need the ability to be angry and aggressive where indignation and aggressiveness are appropriate. Able to be kindly and loving and tolerant in the normal course of their daily lives.

They will need whatever heritage of hope and faith we can bequeath them. They will need to know from us that people can still have moments of vivid enjoyment and times of relaxation and thoughtfulness and calm.

Because we know that our leadership is more important than ever before, we worry more when we feel a child of ours growing away from us. We are more bewildered still when we see him manifesting traits of which we disapprove. We ask ourselves anxiously what makes him so moody? What makes him standoffish? Too forward? Too timid? Too tempestuous? Too meek?

We wonder: Why does there seem at times to be a chasm widening between us? Why does he look down on us and tell us virtually that we know nothing? What can we do to get him over acting as if *he* knew it all?

What can we do about his argumentativeness? His sudden withdrawals? What does it mean when he seems so secretive, as

[4]

if he were living his life apart, not wanting to let us in? What about his confidence in us? Just yesterday, it seemed, he depended so on us. Today perhaps a little. Tomorrow not at all. For what is he searching when he wanders away?

A father says: "My kid has me stumped. One day he's reading about world affairs and discussing them like an old man.

Mother, weeping: "What have I done to deserve such treatment?"
Father, comforting: "All you've done is raise a normal adolescent."

The next day, he's tearing up bits of sponge and floating them in the tub like a two-year-old, claiming he's carrying on great experiments. He's a neither-nor. You don't know how to treat him."

A mother says: "My girl's an enigma. One day she demands, 'Why won't you let me do anything on my own?' The next day she's scolding, 'Why won't you do anything with me?' . . . I wish I knew what she really wants."

A son says: "My dad keeps quarterbacking me, and my mom wants me to do everything without *any* reminding. You don't

[5]

know if you're expected to be eight or eighty. It's rough."

A daughter says: "I'm too old to be a squab and too young to be a chicken. What am I? I guess a dead duck, that's all."

Each young one speaks according to his own lights, prompted by his own feelings. Yet each after his own fashion is saying the same things:

> These are the years when the pull backward and the push forward are at a tug of war with each other . . .

> These are the years when we are wishing for yet fearing the things to come.

As for us—we, the parents, are looking forward to our children's growing up, yet we fear the separation. We are hoping that they will gradually form boy-girl contacts, yet we fear that the demon sex may move in too quickly and that they will lose their sense of proportion and hurdle too many barriers too fast.

YOUR CHILD'S FEELINGS ARE IMPORTANT

Your adolescent may put on bravado or an I-don't-care manner. He may appear callous and noncommittal, as if nothing you do makes any impression. But underneath he reacts keenly. He is at an age when his feelings are heightened and quickened.

Many times he is reacting with surges of feeling within him bigger than he can comfortably manage. They frighten him. And so, he tries often to cover up *to himself* as well as to you what he feels. His I-don't-careness is one of his coverings. His air of how-big-I-am is another. Actually he is deeply desirous of having you understand.

Many times he is daydreaming and fantasying inside him. He is stretching reality beyond its boundaries, visioning ahead into the future, often with mistaken ideas born out of the past. And strange though this may sound to you—it is often

[6]

*these mistaken ideas and fantasies which prompt him in how
he behaves.*

Take Tina, who has just turned fifteen. Her father had
been killed in action during World War II. When Tina was
five, petite, alive, and full of dancing, her mother had had a
boy friend. Evening after evening when this big man came
over, Tina would whirl and twirl in giddy excitement, as delighted as her mother and showing it more openly, in the
thrill of having a man around again like the daddy she had
last seen when she was three. She would grow gigglier and
sillier and wilder in her attempts to capture his attention.

"Don't be so silly, Tina," her mother would chide.

"Hey, girl, calm down. Do you want to scare me away?" the
boy friend would banter.

Then came a sad day when the big man no longer came to
take mother out. Tina didn't know that he and her mother
had decided that they didn't fit together. Tina at five mistakenly imagined that the wildness for which she was chided
and her glee in having a man around were the cause of his
going.

At fifteen Tina had forgotten the whole incident. But whenever she met a boy who called forth small stirrings of excitement in her she would suddenly become aloof and condescend-
ing.

"I could brain her," her mother complained. "She's pretty
as a picture. And yet when she freezes up that way she's left out
of half the parties. I get furious at her. But I get even more
furious at myself. What have I done wrong to make her like
this?"

From Tina: "I don't know what it is. I just can't loosen up
or talk or laugh or be gay when I'm with boys . . ."

Deep down inside her she unconsciously feared that if she
were gay or giddy or silly, they would leave . . .

Like Tina's mother, parents today are apt to blame them-

[7]

selves for almost everything. They dwell on the mistakes they think they have made. They berate themselves unduly, not knowing that often a *youngster's imaginings cause a lot of his trouble*.

What was holding Tina back were her fantasies based on old, forgotten and mistaken imaginings. But her mother's irritation at her only made matters worse. As her mother came to understand that the fear of imagined things was blocking Tina, she grew more warmly sympathetic. In place of the push of mother condemnation, Tina gained the backing of mother love to help her through.

In adolescence many old unsolved fears crop up more frighteningly. Many old wishes stir more disturbingly. Many old imaginings press more vividly. Those of us who live and work with children need to understand the drives and wishes and fears that commonly propel them. Then, when a youngster behaves in ways that now seem inexplicable, we shall be able to say to ourselves, "Look, he isn't doing these things to spite me. Nor is he necessarily failing because I've been a failure. His faulty behavior isn't necessarily a result of faulty handling. I've made mistakes, naturally. But he is also in the grip of mistaken ideas. These have entered into making him do the foolish, frightened, unthinkable things he does. Since I see that I'm not all to blame, I feel less defensive and more sympathetic and tolerant."

This is heartening. As more of us realize that the blame for everything big and small does not have to rest on our shoulders, we can breathe a deep sigh, spread our arms wide and lift our heads higher. This frees us, in turn, to focus more profoundly on what we want for our child.

THESE THINGS WE WANT

We want to help each teen-ager of ours grow into the best person he can possibly be.

[8]

We want to understand him as a maturing individual, taking into account his potentialities, not pushing him but helping him to move ahead.

We want to learn better how to allow him enough freedom for growth of the independence which he needs to assume bit by bit.

We want to become sensitive to how he may be misinterpreting facts and imagining things and then building on what he imagines rather than on what is actually true. For in this way we shall be able to see more clearly where he needs help in setting himself straight.

We want to know how to provide adequate guideposts and adequate boundary lines so that he does not go too far and do unwise things which might get him into trouble.

We want to know enough about our own hopes and fears and expectations to prevent these from causing unnecessary conflict between us and inadvertently getting in the way of what we are sincerely striving to do for him.

Toward these ends, we shall need to lay the groundwork on two great corner stones.

UNDERSTANDING OUR CHILD'S FEELINGS
and
UNDERSTANDING OUR OWN FEELINGS
These are the firmest
foundations for
SUCCESS
in
bringing him up.

Curiously, we build the first best when we build the second first. Then the structure of our relationship rises all the more solidly and the major problems of living with our teen-agers are well on their way to being solved.

[9]

2. Your Feelings Are Important

Uppermost in a parent's feelings these days lies our own concern over the ever-present problem of *authority*. We are eager to give our teen-ager enough responsibility but we fear giving him too much leeway. We know he must develop independence. And yet we fear that he may get out of hand and out of control. We have heard so much talk about the necessity for parents (and for teachers) to give adolescent children *freedom* that we often hesitate to step in. Then when we do step in to assume authority we are often afraid that what we are doing is wrong.

Actually during most of his teens, this teen-ager of ours still needs us to rely on.

> He still needs
> OUR FIRMNESS
> to help him stand
> MORE FIRMLY HIMSELF.

Some forbiddings, restrictions and demands are bound to enter in home, in school and in other groups where he finds himself.

"I hate to put the brakes on, but I have to," one woman remarked. "There's a bunch of thirteen-year-olds in the neighborhood and they congregate at our place. When they get to roughhousing and to throwing the couch pillows around and spilling Coke and soda pop over the rugs, I have to call a halt."

Says another to her seventeen-year-old: "I can't have you and your friends burning holes in the furniture. We can't afford new upholstery every few months."

"No, Son," says a father, "I'm not willing to have you play football, with that knee of yours."

"No matter how important that party is, and I know it's terribly important, you're running a temp, dear, and you've got to stay home."

"No. We are not going to let you use the car if you get another ticket for careless driving."

"I don't care what others do, Daughter, but I don't believe in a sixteen-year-old girl dating with a twenty-two-year-old fellow."

As in the old days when he was little, three rules must still reign:

> This is important for health and safety.
> This is important to protect property.
> This is important because of law and order and social acceptability.

These are firm bases for standing firm. Actually, however, they do not enter into too many of the issues that confront us. And this is fortunate because *when the burden of forbiddings, restrictions and demands overbalances the chances for independent action, a child loses self-confidence.* He either becomes *afraid* to act or he becomes *rebellious*.

On many more occasions another issue enters. When we step in with the authoritarian voice, we are frequently saying:

This is important because it's important to ME!

If we are altogether honest, a great many of the issues that arise are important actually for this reason and for this reason mainly. We want a thing done because *we* feel the way we do about it.

This does not mean, however, that we should wave our desires aside. They're an essential part of the picture. They must be taken into account. When we frankly consider our own feelings, we put ourselves in a much stronger position than when we claim that they have little to do with what we ask.

"But," admitted one mother, " 'way down inside me I'm ashamed of insisting on anything for my own sake. Somehow I feel I have no right to want what I want. So I start selling myself a bill of goods. I tell myself that my children have to mind because it's good for children to mind. Actually, however, I know that's nonsense. It makes me into a dictator when the days of dictatorship should be past. Then, because I'm divided inside and feeling guilty, I get irritated and irritable and picky and I wobble uncertainly and I'm not effective at all."

"While I," her husband put in, "I'm the opposite. The less justified I feel in wanting things my way the more justified I act. I become a regular bully. I pound the table and grow insistent. I see now what I'm doing. I'm covering my real feelings with a lot of shouting. And I end by getting my children's revolt."

Most of us want what we want because we want it. But we manage to find ways of hiding this. Shades of our childhood rise in us. Old prohibitions reecho: "Don't be selfish or self-centered. Don't think of yourself. Think of others, my dear." In consequence, we are seldom honest or free in declaring our wants.

Instead we may rake up a high pile of grievances to justify our demands. "You never use your head so I have to use mine for you." We may heap up proof that a child is too young to know what to do. "So he needs us to *tell* him from the vantage point of our superior age and experience." We keep pushing relatively unimportant reasons to the fore. And we think more of them simply because they make us appear to be thinking less of ourselves.

Obviously this is folly. A far more productive policy is to try to be honest.

"You will have to make your bed before you leave for school in the morning. It gets under my skin to have it left undone all day." This is a very different thing from saying, "Unless you learn to make your bed as you should, you won't know how to take care of your own home properly when you get married." In the former, you are being more honest about your feelings. You are admitting that it's for *you* you're asking. You're not putting on an act that it's for your child.

He may still scold at you roundly. But basically he will love and respect you far more for being honest than he will if he senses any sham. In the long run, knowing that you are open and square with him wins cooperation to a far greater degree than many a more reasonable "reason" that is essentially less sincere.

It does no good to pretend you don't want a thing because you feel that wanting it is no good. You may fool yourself often, but you don't often fool him.

YOUR FEELINGS SPEAK LOUDER
than what you
SAY OR DO.

Just as surely as a horseback rider communicates uncertainty to his horse no matter how much he tries to hide it, so do we communicate our feelings to the youngsters whom we guide.

One night Tom's father listened to a lecturer say that it was unwise to put too much emphasis on school grades. "Some children do better in one field than another. Some do better manually; some mechanically. Some are working up to capacity at a B level; some at a C level. Not everybody can get all A's. Nor are all A's important for everybody. A child doesn't need all A's to be successful in life. What he does need is to feel that his parents—and his teachers—are with him, all A's or not."

Tom's father had nodded and had said to himself: "Yes, that sounds right."

Next day Tom brought home his report card. As usual, he'd been strong in shop and "manual skills" and weak in what he called "that highbrow stuff."

His father, however, remained obedient to the precept he was trying to follow. He looked the card over and handed it back with a casual air.

Neither spoke.

Tom's father went on drawing at his pipe. Tom sat ganglylegged, shoving his feet on the carpet, back and forth, until he finally blurted out, "I didn't do such a good job."

"We-ell," from his father calmly but with a speeded up puffing in and out. "It's a good enough card, Tom." But underneath he didn't feel it was. He *did* care despite his effort to hide this from himself and from Tom.

Tom sensed it. The discrepancy between what his father felt and what his father said bothered him. As he put it to his counselor later, "I knew he wanted to say, 'If you don't do better, you'll never be a success.' He tries not to push but he pushes too much . . ."

And then Tom came out with a profound truth: "You can push with silence as much as with noise." His father's feelings had spoken louder than his words.

Tom was angry. "If he pushes, I'll push back. He's dishonest, that's what he is. I'll be damned if I'll work from now on. I'll be damned if I'll do anything to please him!"

Rodney's father, in contrast, was more honest. He had heard the same lecture. He too had said, "That's a good idea."

Like Tom, Rodney was strong in mechanical abilities. He was also good in sports. As usual the rest of his card was only fair.

Rodney's father started off by saying, "It doesn't really matter." But then he changed his tune. "Yes, Rod, it does . . .

"That guy who lectured said you shouldn't care too much about your kid's grades as long as he's working. And you work plenty hard. I know I shouldn't want you to get all A's but I do . . . Why, I wonder? There are things in life besides grades."

"Football, for instance," Rodney ventured.

"That's what I counted on when I was your age," Rodney's father answered.

"You were team captain . . ."

"Uh-huh, but what did it net me?"

"You talk about it enough."

"I know."

Rodney's father seemed puzzled but he went on thinking out loud. "It was no use hitching my wagon to a football. It let me down plenty. *I* counted on it, but the profs got my number as a numskull and I flunked out of college . . . I guess when I said grades weren't important I was trying to fool you, just like I was trying to fool myself. I still wish I'd done better . . ."

"Okay, Dad, okay!" Rodney countered a little impatiently. "I see your point. Only don't push me to make up for not pushing yourself when you were young. I've told you I want to go to work and not to college, so let me be."

Rodney's father nodded and smiled a broad, quiet smile. "The grades don't matter. You're okay, kid." It had the right sound now, clear as a bell when he said it. He felt it, that was why. His feeling and words were one.

As Rodney went out he smiled an answering smile shyly back at his father, and suddenly his father knew profoundly there was one thing that did matter more than grades. He and his boy were friends.

At times our feelings are such that we cannot share them. We don't always have to. But neither need we dissemble. We can always admit, *"I'm bothered by something inside me; not by you."* This proves immeasurably relieving for the teen-ager who is so prone to blame himself.

On the other hand, it's quite possible to use our feelings to make our children go our way more than is helpful or fair to them. Like a girl who sheds tears to get a lover to do her bidding. We then play on a child's heartstrings and get him to be a yes man too often for his own good.

It is also quite possible to give in to our own wishes too often. Then the load of demands grows so big our children rebel at everything. Then, if we want them to do something really important, they still will renege.

By giving more thought to our own wishes, we can often prevent such an impasse. By giving ourselves due attention, we often become able to forgo some of our wishes more peacefully than we anticipate and without as much sense of sacrificing what we believe is right.

"You know," said one father, "I used to say, 'What's right is right and under no circumstances am I going to let my children by-pass it.' But since I've taken my own wishes into the picture more honestly, I see that I often call things right simply because they are right-er for *me*."

It doesn't make us lose caste to change our minds. It doesn't hurt, for instance, to say, "Skip it, Jane. It isn't necessary after all to stop at the store for me. I forgot you had a club meeting this afternoon. I was thoughtless to ask."

Another thing that can help immeasurably is to bring our own adolescence to bear on the wishes we have for our children. The thinking-back process can make for "less pressurizing," to use one youngster's phrase.

We know we can't handle our teen-agers precisely as we were handled. Times have changed. The world has changed. Children are different. We are different. But in many "feeling" respects still the same.

Most of us see our adolescent children with bewilderment carried over from our own adolescence. Because of our own puzzled feelings about ourselves as we were *then,* we often feel puzzled about our children *now.* Remembering what our feelings were *then* can help clarify our feelings *now.* And this in turn helps us act more wisely. Just as Rodney's father benefited by recapturing how he felt when he was young, so can we in many instances.

By true regard for the
FEELINGS WE HAD IN OUR OWN ADOLESCENCE
we gain truer regard for
OUR ADOLESCENT'S FEELINGS
right now.

It is not easy to recapture exactly how we felt. We can get at memories, perhaps, of being too fat, too thin, too tall, too short. Memories, perhaps, of various uncomfortable moments. Of being unable to be convincing when we wanted most to convince. Of being unable to be attractive when we wanted most to attract. Too eager, perhaps. Or too bungling. Dreaming about things to come and shamefaced about our dreaming. Wondering about life and trying not to wonder. Feeling old, terribly old.

"Like our children now! And being treated terribly young!"

"Why do we smile when we think of ourselves as adolescents?" a group of parents asked themselves.

"Perhaps out of charity."

"To tell ourselves that feelings we had then were nonexist-

[17]

ent, especially the sex feelings, because we thought them so bad."

"Or we smile to pass over the memory of having wanted to flaunt those feelings . . ."

"And to forget that we had the revolt feelings too . . ."

"What do you mean, the revolt feelings?"

Mother: "Didn't I tell you to clean up?"
Daughter: "But I did an hour ago! Can't you see the difference?"

"The hostile feelings *against* our parents when we felt they were old-fashioned and foolish and didn't know anything."

"You mean, when we thought that we knew it all . . ."

"We didn't like to see certain feelings in ourselves then. We don't like to see them in our adolescents now. The sex feelings and the hostile feelings, those were the worst. They still are."

Ask yourself: Do you remember your feelings toward your parents? Your struggles to break loose? Your worried resent-

[18]

ments when you felt they were holding the reins too tight? Your sorry anger when you felt what to you spelled a lack of support?

Do you remember your feelings toward your bodies? Your feelings toward girls if you were a boy and toward boys if you were a girl? Your feelings about love and marriage? Your wonderings about sex and sex contact and birth?

As you read this book you will be reminded of these questions again and again. If you remember little, perhaps as you read you will remember more. You may come upon things that will make you exclaim, "I'd forgotten about that!" Or "Oh, I see! I, too, must have felt that way without realizing it then."

We have buried so much. Sometimes even while an event was happening, we shoveled its most important meanings under the soil of consciousness, because inside of us it touched old feelings of fear or hesitance, guilt or shame. Even so, it still can propel us to meet our children's feelings with unnecessary fear and hesitance, with uncalled-for guilt and shame.

The more we can recapture those young feelings of ours with clarity, with honesty and without too great a sense of apology, the more shall we grow in acceptance and understanding of our children. The more shall we be able to know and learn about them. The better able shall we be to help them grow and mature.

LIVING WITH YOUR CHILDREN

When you find out that something is *natural* in your child which you thought was *naughty,* you can breathe more easily . . .

When you find that some feeling in you is *normal* that you thought was not, you can take things in better spirit . . .

When you get some concrete and practical examples and principles, and some help and guidance, you can feel more assured.

LIVING WITH YOUR TEEN-AGER does not mean giving up life for him. Living WITH does not mean only living FOR. Living *for*—when it stands alone by itself—by itself brings sacrifice. Living *with* brings fruition on both sides—on his and on yours.

In its best sense it means caring about and considering one another, accepting imperfections, mistakes and uncertainties. Living through the battling moments, not trying to evade them. Acquiring increasing sympathy for the impatient and irritable and irrational moments. Acquiring the ability to communicate strength and love through the struggling and unhappy moments that inevitably come. Enjoying the high moments, and cherishing the quiet moments of peace.

A teen-ager said cynically, "Parents are people who try to help you but don't know you well enough to do so."

Your goal is to be another kind of parent. One who helps his children realistically by knowing and understanding them well.

By now you have glimpsed that understanding of him involves also understanding of yourself.

Your feelings and his feelings are continuously jostling and meshing with each other.

The hopes you have had for yourself meet constantly with the hopes you have for him.

The doubts you have had about yourself meet with your doubts about him.

Your old and new fears and your old and new imaginings often press unrealistically into your relationship with him.

Out of your own youth you bring a wealth of memories to bear on his youth. Reevaluating these may take away some of your fears for him. They may enable you the better to feel *with* him, the vantage point of your adulthood giving you a greater sense of ease and steadiness with which to help him move more steadily through his tremulous reachings to become an adult.

By accepting yourself more confidently as an adult who has once also been an adolescent, you may come to accept him more warmly, thus helping him gain fuller confidence in himself.

For these reasons, this book will talk not only about your teen-ager but about *you*.

3. The Strivings That Drive Him

"I keep wondering: What is he after?" a parent asked thoughtfully.

"What is he driving at? What is he striving for?"

THE EMOTIONAL FOODS THAT HE CRAVES

If you are struggling to make a dress fit properly, or if you are trying to make a table top balance evenly on the four legs you have built and you simply cannot attain what you are after, what happens? You're apt to grow exasperated. Perhaps you throw the job over in disgust. Perhaps you put it aside resignedly. Perhaps you attack it with open anger or with anger held in behind gritted teeth. Comes a measure of success, however, and you settle down to more steady progress without the waste of good humor and energy that the struggle with continuous failure entailed. But these are relatively small things for you to be after.

Far bigger, for instance, is your wish for greater achievements, like doing a job well or raising your children. Bigger, too, is your wish to have your spouse love you dearly. These are among the more important things you are after. They grow out of the deep need for certain basic emotional foods that all human beings must have to nourish them from birth on.

[22]

To be healthy and sound we need emotional nourishments as surely as we need physical foodstuffs.

We need *love* in good measure, and we need to give it. We need to feel that we are *wanted and belong*. We need to feel that we are capable of *adequate achievement* so that we can manage to meet life's demands. We need *recognition* for what we achieve. We need to know that the *pleasure which our senses and our body can bring us* is permissible and good and that our enjoyment does not make us "bad." We need to feel *accepted and understood*. And finally we need to feel *worth while and essentially worthy in being uniquely the self that we are.*

These things we strive for continuously in terms of the time of life at which we find ourselves. Take affection, for instance. When we were tiny only one person's love really mattered. That was mother's. Gradually father's moved to close second. Somewhat later, if you were a girl, father's affection became top requirement. All through childhood, even though other people came into view, your parents stood highest. But gradually during adolescence things changed. Outsiders came to matter more. Chums. Friends. Heroes. Crushes. Sweethearts. And finally a cherished partner to share love with, and children to love.

The gearing in of love needs with partner and children belongs to an adult stage of life. We need to reach adulthood before we can marry. The same ways of satisfying the same emotional hungers would be out of place, say, at five and fifteen. The early teen-ager is not ready to have his love needs satisfied in the same manner as are we. Just so with the various strivings that drive him. They must be geared in with gaining the needed emotional foodstuffs by means which are not only fitting to his stage of development but also fitting to what the culture dictates as suitable for his particular age. He goes after his satisfactions in terms more compatible with *his* time of life.

[23]

"Any sign of approval from Pete's cronies is more important to him than his father's or mine."

"All Sally looks for is a pat on the back from her art teacher. She doesn't care a bit whether we like those horrors she paints."

"I'm out. Bill's aim in life is to be liked by his big hero, the swimming coach at the Y."

Our teen-ager still wants love and our love is still essential to him. He still wants recognition and ours is still important. But he is struggling to move, as he must, from a place where eventually we who are now the center of his family and universe give up our place. He must find a new center composed of himself and a partner who together create a new family and a new world.

He has a long trek to travel from early adolescence to reach his new world. He needs to learn through actually doing it that he can make his own friends outside his family. He needs to belong to groups of his own choosing with whom he feels kinship and who choose him in return. He has to measure himself with other male folk and feel liked by them in order to honor himself eventually as a man in his own right—not only as a boy in his family. He has to try out a number and a variety of contacts with female folk and again learn through experience that he is accepted and liked by them also before he will be ready to make a sound and intimate choice of a mate. He needs to know deeply that others like him. But he will be a sorry failure if he turns for this solely to us.

And so, if he were able to put very simply one thing he is after in terms of his life strivings at this particular age and stage, he would say:

I want others to like me.

. . . I want you to like me—yes. But not you alone!

His inner and healthy intention now is to widen the circle of those who like and accept him. For this reason his interest will be more intensely focused away from you onto those others whom he so greatly needs.

Closely linked with this wish to be liked by others comes

FATHER'S DILEMMA
"Why on earth did her mother ask *me* to fetch her home?"

another thing he is after. Were he to phrase this second striving of his he would say:

> I want to be like others.

. . . Especially do I want to identify with others of my own age!

In his early teens when he is beginning to separate himself from his family, the wish to be like others of his own age and sex comes most emphatically to the fore. He is bent on dressing like them, talking like them, walking like them, eating like them. He will balk mightily if we place on his shoulders requirements or restrictions that "those others" don't have.

"Moth-er!" says young daughter, shaking her head most em-

[25]

phatically. "You *can't* go with me to that party. None of the other mothers do."

"Gee," says young son, with a hoisting of those perpetually down-slipping levis, "I wish you'd quit pestering me to wear a belt. I told you, it just isn't done."

"I can't take a thermos of hot vegetables to school for lunch! They'd think I was sick!"

By being like others his own age he feels he *belongs*. He is one of them. He and they together form a kind of collective, many-headed, many-armed, many-legged version of himself. He is no longer just one helpless child but twenty children, and in numbers lies strength.

It's as if he were thinking: "In my first bungling attempts to become a person in my own right with an identity of my own, I feel safer and surer when I see a lot of other me's walking and running around. I feel safer right now being a *they-me* than a *me-me*. As I look at another blue-jeaned me, or at another me in a white scarf tied peasant-fashion like on fifty other me's, I feel more rightfully confirmed not only in my blue-jeanedness or my white-scarfedness, but also in my long-armedness and in the bigger-nosedness that has recently come so bonily onto my face.

"But being a me like all these other still bungling me's isn't quite enough. In addition I need something bigger and better to pattern after . . ." And so he picks heroes as well as gangs.

Away down inside him, however, he still needs you also to identify with. Essentially he has patterned after you these many years and he still does it in many ways. In some respects Junior still wants to be like Dad. In some respects he also wants to be like Mother. In case you don't know it, this is a heritage you bequeath him that lasts in some measure all through his life. By being like you, he *is* you to himself. He will carry you in this fashion into his own home with him.

Even after you are gone, he will still have in him some of your fortifying values and strengths.

Though he is temporarily bent upon opposition, just give him time. Only pray that he won't turn out to be too faithful a reproduction of you. Or of his own "gang" either. To be healthy he needs to be more than a mere reproduction. He needs also to be an individual, able to stand up at times in opposition and defend what to him is necessary or desirable. "If you kids plan to sneak into the show without tickets, don't count on me as part of the crowd. I don't want to do it and won't." Taking such action calls for individual courage. In order to do it a youngster must feel himself a person in his own right.

And so, as your young one moves through his teens you will probably notice him going after the attainment of selfhood and integrity. You will probably notice many things which say for him: I want my own identity . . .

I want to be like myself.
. . . Not a repetition or duplicate of anyone else . . .
. . . With a sense of having my own kind of special quality and personality . . .
. . . With trust in myself to be myself . . .
. . . With independence that is not a revolt from dependency and so does not have to disregard interdependence . . .

These are great things and hard things to come by, with many hazards along the road. But once achieved, they bring with them the wish you will finally see coming through:

I want to like others.
. . . I need to establish intimacy and to feel the expansion of solid friendship.
. . . I need intimacy, too, that possesses the warmth and affection spoken with touch and body language, not only with mind's meeting and words. Eventually I will hope to have this

grow into a tender and concentrated love for my mate and my children so that I may give myself to them without fear of losing myself as I give.

. . . More broadly, I hope to be able to like people of all ages and colors and creeds without intolerance creeping in. I hope to be able to like those who are different from me as well as those who are similar to me. I hope that the liking of others will be broad and embracing so that I do not see the faces of enemies where I might be seeing the faces of friends.

In order to achieve these four things he is after, our teen-ager must also achieve a mighty fifth. If he were able to put this last into simple words he would say:

I want to like myself.

This wish is pivotal, as we'll see in a few moments.

Meanwhile let's list his strivings all together. And, since the last which we've mentioned is the most essential, let's put it right at the top.

Here they stand then, all five:

I want to LIKE MYSELF!
I want OTHERS TO LIKE ME!
I want TO BE LIKE OTHERS!
I want to BE LIKE MYSELF!
I want to LIKE OTHERS
and be able to love deeply and well!

It is obvious that your adolescent isn't actually able to put his strivings into just these words. In stating them we have put together many of the separate things he desires. If you were to ask your younger teen-ager, for instance, "What is it you want?" he would probably give you quite different answers. For example:

"I want a bigger allowance."

"Why?"

"So I can do more what the others do" . . . that is, be more like them . . . or "So I can treat them to shows and stuff" . . . namely, so I can get them to like me more . . .

"I want a cashmere sweater and saddle shoes."

"Why?"

"Because all the other girls have them." . . . Again the wish to be one of the group.

Or "I want to be top skier in our club" . . . both so they will like me and I will like myself . . .

As you notice the wishes that crop up in your individual boy or girl you will see that ultimately they too are expressions of one or more of the big five. As you watch with sensitivity you will see furthermore that your child's liking of himself is the number one essential.

THE TOP REQUIREMENT IS FEELING WORTH WHILE

The greatest task in growing up is to weather the time and tide and the changes that come, all the while maintaining an inner sense of being worthy and worth while.

Unless a person can like himself securely, he is bound to feel uncertain of others' liking him. It's as if he kept wondering, "How can others like me when I feel so unlikable and 'bad'?"

Unless he can like himself securely, he is apt to get mixed up in his strivings and many unfortunate things can result. He may, for instance, grow rough and tough to gain status. Like Jock, the leader of a marijuana "gang," he may throw himself into sensational escapades to feel "great." Or else, like poor, timid Freddie, he may "lick boots" and try to be just a shadow of the boys he goes with, unconsciously figuring, "If I'm exactly like them, perhaps then they'll like me." He expects to find himself this way. Actually he loses himself. He is swallowed up in the crowd and never develops his feeling of selfhood. And so, he never arrives at the place where he can truly like others and love deeply. For, *having forfeited his own identity, he does not have himself to give*.

> A person
> CANNOT LIKE OTHERS
> and give love deeply
> UNLESS HE LIKES HIMSELF.

You know this from your own experience. In moments when you are conscious of not liking yourself, what do you do? For one thing, you may grow disgruntled and moody, timid, standoffish. You feel unfriendly to the world. For another thing, you may cringe when you meet others. You may try to placate them. You hope they will smooth your back and soothe you. Your emphasis is on getting them to make you happy, not on loving them and on making them happy. Your focus is on yourself, not on them.

The person who feels truly acceptable, worth while and worthy is not defensive. He isn't punitive. He is more assured and more courageous. He is more able to give himself to others without fear of being lost in them. His wish to give himself can become a reality instead of a dream.

When he feels secure in his own self-regard, he can submerge himself and identify with others without feeling threatened. He can suffer denials without feeling that he's being punished because he's been "bad." He can be generous without needing aggrandizement to feel worth more.

Everyone is bound to have moments of not liking himself. But in adolescence, with its increased pressures from without and its increased stirrings from within, self-loathing and depression can readily take over. Self-liking and the wholesome gladness of being alive can be lost.

Shall we say, then, that the *greatest task* the adolescent has to accomplish in growing up is to gain an identity—or self-hood—which he feels is WORTHY and WORTH WHILE.

. . . Not one for which he must apologize.

. . . Not one on which he must look down.

. . . Rather a selfhood which he can value, honor and regard.

He must feel worthy of being loved. Worthy of being wanted and of belonging in closeness with others. He must feel worth while enough to know that he can achieve according to his abilities and attain recognition for what he achieves.

He must know that the pleasure which his senses and his body crave with youthful compulsion does not make him unworthy. That the sensations which course through his blood so warmly do not make him "bad."

He must know that NONE of the feelings he has is too terrible. That NO feelings can destroy him or shatter his worthiness. That no matter how monstrous he may believe them to be at the moment, his feelings still are human and natural enough to be accepted and understood.

He must be so confirmed in his essential worth that regardless of how he feels, he still knows he is strong enough to keep his behavior under control.

To repeat and to sum up:

Your adolescent needs to feel
WORTH WHILE AND WORTHY—
"GOOD"—NOT "BAD".

He will BE "GOOD" more readily as he FEELS "GOOD" inside.

And yet, for many reasons which we shall presently go into, your adolescent no doubt carries in him too many feelings of being condemnable. These make it harder for you to control him and harder for him to control himself.

Helping him get over these feelings is of foremost importance. It is the number one aid in helping him to engage in good and positive actions.

As he feels more worth while and worthy, he is able to do more worth-while and worthy things. He is happier and can make others happier—including you.

Helping your adolescent
FEEL HE'S A "GOOD" PERSON—
This is a good and worth-while task.

It is, however, a complex task. For many of the feelings of being "good" or "bad" took root in early childhood. Some sprang up at the very start of life—in the days when a child was even too little to talk.

To understand him now, we shall, therefore, need to glimpse how he felt then. We shall need to trace, at least briefly, how his feelings about himself began.

4. It Helps to Know How Troubles Start

To understand and help our teen-ager's actions, we need to understand the feelings from his past and his present that push him and make him do what he does. Particularly do we need to understand his feelings about himself. These color his behavior more than anything else.

ADOLESCENT PROBLEMS STRETCH 'WAY BACK

Almost always, liking or not liking oneself reaches back into childhood's first five or six years. Old feelings carried over in the unconscious mind crop out in adolescent feelings of self-belittlement, in feelings of being unworthy and "bad." Many of these old feelings, then, join with feelings which are rising freshly at this time of life.

In the beginning, as far as the baby is concerned, everything has to do with his body. Your baby, like other babies, craved nothing so much as the body satisfactions that came with being cuddled and fed. Perhaps, though, 'way back when he was cradle size he was told, "No, no!" if he made hungry demands, since the belief then held that it was necessary to feed babies by the clock. If he cried, craving the body pleasure of feeding at an off-scheduled time, he was "bad." And so one of the first snapshot impressions he got of himself left a mind picture:

Baby is "bad" for wanting
BODY PLEASURE.

Furthermore, because he failed to get the emotional nourishment he needed, baby grew angry. Perhaps he screamed, and he was scolded or in some fashion greeted with irritation. This made a second mind picture:

Baby is "bad" for
BEING MAD.

A little while later when he was toilet-trained, again focus was on his body.

To a small child elimination is a great achievement. It is also a pleasurable act. Watch a baby having an evacuation. His whole body wriggles in delight. If we made him feel he was dirty, or if we imposed toilet training on him so early that he was uncomfortable trying to do what we asked before muscles and mind were quite ready, we took enjoyment away from him.

He wanted to go on performing his body functions for a while, at least until his muscles were readier, in more primitive and pleasurable fashion. So again anger arose. And again came the two pictures: baby is "bad" for wanting body pleasure of such a primitive nature, and baby is "bad" for being mad.

As he went on, other body pleasures may also have come into the field and were interfered with. Possibly his thumb was taken out of his mouth when sucking it felt good to him, or body explorations that felt pleasant were stopped in the belief that this was necessary.

[34]

Coupled with these things, you also had to do things that were unpleasant or painful when he was hurt or sick.

In his mind he may have put these various happenings together. As many children do, he may have added them up in his own fancy and in his own fashion to mean, quite mistakenly, that your ministrations were a kind of punishment. Then the picture in his mind was blown up to enlarged dimensions. He was sure he was "bad."

He wanted his pleasure and he wanted to bring out his anger.

But he wanted also to avoid your displeasure.

He grew afraid of his body with its "bad" impulses. He might lose you if he showed his feelings. He was in a corner. He had to do something about himself.

By this time he wished to pattern himself after you and in a way *be* you. This offered him one "out." He gradually became a kind of mother or father to himself. Even when he was quite little, after you said "No, no!" to him, you may have noticed him going around shaking his head and saying "No, no!" to himself. He was being you even then. But he became more you as he grew. And here more trouble may have entered the scene.

In his imagined badness, he often fancied that you were more of an ogre than you were in reality. He became more condemnatory and stricter with himself than you ever were with him. And he often resented you mightily for what he imagined you were. He hated you soundly for it. This added itself to his former anger. And he hated himself for hating you.

He hated himself and he feared himself also. He feared what his hostility made him impulsively want to do. For inside of himself his anger was shaping primitive fantasies of revenge. Perhaps he was wishing to bite and devour or to soil and smear and use his body as a weapon in any way that he

[35]

could. Then he blamed himself doubly for his feelings and more than ever felt himself "bad."

This much for the story of how it began—his feeling of not liking himself. Away back it started from two rugged roots: He was bad because of the push of his body for pleasure. He was bad because of the push of his hostile urges. The sense of not liking himself spread then apace with the branching out of imaginings as these grew from the two roots planted in his earliest years.

To put this more tersely:

> ANGER and the
> WISH FOR BODY PLEASURE
> lie at the base of
> FEELING "BAD."

WHETHER FACT OR FANCY

Many parents and teachers and others dealing with children have known for quite a long time that the early experiences we've been talking of do bring influence to bear on later behavior.

What they have not known clearly, however, is that *it is not alone the actual happenings that count.* It's *how a child takes what happens* and *what he makes of it in his mind.*

It is true, for instance, that if a child has been loved enough by his parents earlier, he will find it easier now to like himself. Still, it is possible for him to be loved and yet to imagine he isn't.

To cite an extreme case in point, Clarke's mother gave her life for him and yet Clarke grew up feeling she had not loved him. It had happened this way.

One day, when Clarke was three, he was playing on the sidewalk with his ball while his mother sat watching him on the front steps of their home. Suddenly, in a split second, the ball rolled into the street, Clarke dashed after it, and a car swerved around the corner. Quick as a flash, Clarke's mother ran out and shoved her baby roughly out of the way.

The brakes screeched. The car slid. But too late. Clarke's mother was struck, and died the next evening.

What had happened was one thing. What Clarke fantasied about it was another. His mother had pushed him. He imagined this showed anger and bespoke a lack of love. After all, hadn't she told him repeatedly not to run into the street? He fancied she'd been rough because he'd been naughty. And on top of this she had died and left him for good. He must indeed have been very "bad."

Many times, many children take lesser cues and interpet them as fancifully. Many times this starts in the first days of life.

No matter how much we thought we showed love to a baby, the baby himself may have felt that it was not enough. Different babies have different love requirements just as they have different food requirements. *What is enough to nourish one baby is not enough to nourish another. Only the baby himself really knows.*

When your particular teen-ager was a baby, he may have *felt* that he had less love than he craved. He may have wanted more holding and cuddling. But he couldn't tell you about this in words and you may not have known what his cry meant to say. And so this may have set off imaginings in him which grew as he grew.

Take Mary as example. Although fourteen, she kept clamoring for her mother to pick her up at school and drive her home. But when her mother was busy she insisted that Mary must take the bus.

One morning after the usual round of arguings, Mary grew furious. Glaring at her mother, she screamed with the malignant imp of hatred sparking from her eyes, "You! I hate you.

You've never really loved me. You've never done anything for me. You've always been a mean old witch."

In telling about the episode later, Mary's mother said, "For an instant I felt very hurt and indignant. But suddenly memories began to flash into my mind. 'Way back in the days when Mary was a baby, her father and I were having an awful struggle financially. I was bothered and absorbed. I know I handled her absent-mindedly on many an occasion. She could well have caught some sort of message going from my muscles to her muscles when I bathed or dressed her, which told her I was abstracted. I'd leave her alone, too, to cry it out when the tears began.

"I remember, as I talk, how angry she got. She had temper tantrums that were dillies until her father and I punished them out of her. But I see she still harbored resentment. Her anger at my not picking her up at school now is worse because it has joined forces with the anger that she had when I didn't pick her up and hold her as much or as tenderly as she needed when she was a baby in order to feel that she was loved.

"What I did with Mary didn't mean that I was a bad parent. I was a worried parent, that's all. Only Mary interpreted it falsely. She imagined what she just threw up to me. She imagined I'd never really loved her. And she hated me for what she imagined much more than for what I actually did."

As a child grows, there are many rules imposed on him which have no rhyme or reason so far as he is concerned. He would rather be messy than clean. He wants to touch and explore and get into everything. However, he has to be trained and his parents have to do the training. Quite naturally, then, he takes them and not other people as the big ogres of denial and demand.

A great many of the child's wishes and thoughts, a great many of his desires and hostilities focus quite naturally then

[38]

on his parents. They are the ones from whom he wants the most satisfactions. They are the ones to whom he feels most hostile. They are the ones around whom the pattern of his feelings and fantasies begins to take shape.

Whether fact or fancy, if a child felt a lack of love or trust or belonging in the beginning of life with his family, he will find it harder in adolescence to feel at home with his peers. If he felt himself a black sheep or an outcast, he will now feel more isolated and alone and less able to be like the friends with whom he wishes to identify. If he felt an inability to achieve what he was asked to do as a small child, he will feel less firm in tackling tasks that can now give him status. If he felt earlier that he could not gain deserved recognition, he will be more fearful now that belittlement may greet his efforts. If he came to feel that pleasurable sensations were condemnable, he will be less able to approach love and sex and marriage freely and with the smooth-flowing assurance that body and spirit can merge.

We need to realize how small slights can strike a child's sensitivities. His feeling unloved may or may not mean that he has been unloved. His feeling unwanted or incapable may not mean that he was unwanted or incapable. Nonetheless *how he himself felt about it originally* and *how his imagination expanded his feelings*—these are of paramount importance.

A CHILD'S FANTASIES AND IMAGININGS
can be MORE IMPORTANT IN SHAPING HIS
ATTITUDES than the ACTUALITY that occurred.

Invariably a child's earlier fantasies enter into the strivings that drive him. They influence his teen-age behavior. They have significant bearing on what he feels about himself and consequently about others.

[39]

Because as a child the teen-ager was too fearful and ashamed of his so-called "bad" feelings and fantasies, he locked many of them up, as it were, and hid them in his unconscious mind. This he did not only to hide them from us but, far more imperatively, to hide them from himself.

But making feelings disappear from view does not make them disappear from existence. They still press. They still push. In one way or another they must come out.

The more fearful or ashamed a child is of them, the more adept will he unconsciously become in protecting himself from seeing them. The more cunningly will he manage to hide what his feelings truly are. The more adroit will he become in going after what he craves in devious, hidden ways and in having feelings come out in forms that keep them unrecognizable to himself and others.

All unconsciously in his childhood he does many such things.

All unconsciously in his teens he still does them.

When he feels "bad," anxious, angry or desirous of what he senses he should not be wanting—he hides by running back, by denying or by disguising through sundry means what he feels.

Let us glimpse how he does these various things.

He runs back

The teen-ager who has felt or imagined that he missed out on emotional nourishments in infancy or childhood may either sit tight in his baby ways or return to them from time to time. In effect he is trying to make up belatedly for things he feels he has missed.

It's as if he were saying to himself, "If I stay young I can perhaps capture what I failed to have enough of earlier," or

[40]

"Maybe if I act like a baby I can get to do now what you didn't let me do enough of then."

He may turn back to striving for satisfactions in ways more childish than befit an adolescent.

"My child," writes a mother, "doesn't seem to want to grow up. She doesn't want to go with girls her own age. She invariably chooses children three or four years younger . . ." Quite obviously, for whatever inner reason she has, this girl is trying to run back to an earlier period.

"My girl," reports another mother, "can't think of anyone but herself. It's not that she seems to think well of herself. She doesn't. I think she's got an awful sense of inferiority. But she always has to hold the center of the stage. She does it by acting silly. She does it by being fresh. She'll even skin a knee or stub a toe if she has to. And she acts so helpless! Everything has to revolve around her every bit of the time."

What better description is there of a baby to whom his whole world is himself and around whom all his world must revolve?

"My boy," a father complains, "is as bright as a whip and still he has to cheat. He keeps copying off the other kids' papers. I asked him why, and do you know what he said? It was the strangest thing. He said, 'It's like tasting from somebody else's plate. When I get the answers off somebody else's paper they seem better to me than when I do them myself.' "

Again the description of a hungry baby is appropriate. This boy goes to his friends as though they were his mother from whom he still is bent on taking more food than he feels he should have. In what he said to his father he disclosed how in his fantasies, albeit unconsciously, this was the sort of act he was playing out. By adding the unethical element to it, he added hostility so that it became an act of sly grabbing with anger concealed except to the eye that reads below the surface.

[41]

He denies

By doing things and developing personality traits which denied the presence of hostile feelings, he could make the hiding act more complete.

EMOTIONAL TAPEWORM—

WANTING MORE OF WHAT HE WANTED MORE OF WHEN HE WAS SMALL

Mother, thoughtfully to herself: "When I see all the things he puts in his mouth now, I wonder if he'd be less greedy if I hadn't kept taking his thumb out when he was small?"

Pretty Deana did this one way. She was so shy and sweet that she automatically saw herself as the dear little darling who wouldn't hurt a fly. Meanwhile she held in the "bad" feelings so tightly that the good feelings didn't come out either. "What's wrong with Deana?" her vexed and bewildered parents asked. "She doesn't give out warmth. She's solitary. She doesn't make any friends."

Tall Charly did it another way. Despite his broad shoulders and finely knit muscles, he couldn't do well in competitive sports. "I keep fumbling," he complained, "instead of connecting up with the ball. I keep missing tackles. Or I stumble or fall at the crucial moment . . ."

Down underneath, Charly was hiding the ugly load of hostility grown so big that he wanted to fight and injure everyone in his path. By stumbling and fumbling and turning awkward he was denying his too-strong, accumulated and hidden impulse to beat and hurt.

Often people go by opposites. Take yourself. Aren't you aware occasionally of being inwardly annoyed although outwardly you put on your nicest manner so as not to show how you actually feel? Sometimes you do this quite consciously. Sometimes, you do it unconsciously.

"I simply can't say 'No' to Johnny," said Johnny's mother. But when she came to know her underneath feelings, she saw that she was hiding and denying her desire to say "No" to Johnny most of the time.

Sue's adoration of a younger sister had always pleased Sue's parents. "Sue's not a bit jealous, bless her. Those books that claim children resent each other are certainly wrong."

But a day arrived when Sue discovered that her ultralovingness had been the opposite of what she had really felt.

He disguises

Inevitably there comes a time when the person finally gives vent to feelings he has previously managed to hide.

With Sue this came when she had a baby and the baby was a girl.

"I can't feed her. I can't dress her. I can't handle her!" She sobbed. "She's so tiny, I seem to be scared."

Sue was scared. But the reason wasn't that the baby was tiny. The hostile feelings toward another little girl baby earlier were coming out now.

By saying, "I can't be nice to the baby!" Sue was disguising the fact that her unconscious emotions were saying, "I won't be nice." By selling herself a reason for acting as she was acting, she hid the real feeling behind the act. That was one disguise she was using. There was also a second.

By removing the hostility from her sister and putting it onto the baby, she was hiding what she had been ashamed and afraid to show her parents earlier. By changing the object of her sentiments, the feelings could come out disguised.

But in spite of all the hiding and disguising, Sue was still afraid and desperately unhappy because of the belated push of the accumulated feelings by which she had come to label herself "bad."

"We've never been an intolerant or prejudiced family, I can't understand Tom's constant remarks about Negroes." . . . "Why on earth should Jed always be late with his papers in school when he's always been so prompt about everything at home?" . . . "Harriet's always been so sweet to her father, why should she be so snippy to boys?"

The answer in each instance may well be that these boys and girls are now letting out in *changed-target disguises*, feelings that they could not let out earlier toward their parents.

They also use the *excuse-giving disguise*.

"I can't get my homework done; that darn teacher piles it on so high!" may be saying "I won't please my parents by doing well." . . . "I can't help necking" may mean "I won't stop doing something I know hurts them." . . . "I feel too tired" may mean "I feel too unwilling to help wash the dishes or clean the house."

But just as Sue felt guilty and miserable in spite of the disguises, so do our own girls and boys. Often they want, in consequence, to punish themselves. And so they often choose a target that permits them *self-punishment* at the same time that it furnishes hostile outlets. Instead of directing hostility onto some outside target, they let it boomerang back onto themselves.

[44]

The boy who failed unnecessarily in school punished his parents incidentally. But primarily he punished himself. The girl who failed to make contacts with boys punished her parents, but even more she punished herself.

That "awful sense of inferiority," that miserable feeling of being no good and worthless, is a kind of self-inflicted torture. So also are repeated *accidents* that seem to have no rhyme nor reason.

"I don't know why Ted keeps smashing the car and getting himself banged up. His eyes and his coordination are perfect and yet he does it time after time . . ."

Of all possible disguises, *illness* is the most convincing.

Medical science today has established that ulcers, allergies, hypertension and other illnesses can have an emotional component.

Take seventeen-year-old Barbara. When she was four an episode occurred that was a kind of on-the-spot illustration of how the disguise through illness works. It was summer and the circus was coming to town, and Barbara's father was going to take her. For weeks ahead Barbara had gazed at the billboards all splendid with elephants and clowns and black, shimmering horses blazoning their promise of the day when she and Daddy would get tickets and peanuts and walk in together proudly to the booming of the band.

When the day finally arrived, Barbara jumped out of bed in excitement. She rushed to her parents' room screeching, "Daddy. Daddy." At the door she stopped.

"Keep quiet, Barbara," her father snapped.

On the bed her mother was moaning. The doctor was bending over her.

Barbara heard long words such as "emergency" and "operation." She didn't comprehend. Nobody noticed her. No one explained. And then Daddy was gone with Mother and the doctor, and the long-faced neighbor lady took Barbara and Barbara's prettiest china doll for company to her house.

That night in the strange bed, Barbara hugged her doll closer and slipped into the forbidden body pleasure of sucking her thumb that, much to Mother's disgust, she had never outgrown.

Remembering back now from her seventeen years of greater wisdom, Barbara tried to talk herself out of the childish pain. "It was an emergency. They couldn't help it." And then, the child sobs caught up with her and the forgotten child fantasies connected with her experience returned.

In her imaginings she had envisioned that somehow Mother had been angry because she and Daddy were going to have fun together. And Mother had taken Daddy from her. And besides, Mother was so disgusted over that old thumb-sucking business that she too had left her. Nobody wanted her. There was no circus, no Daddy, no Mother . . . And she, Barbara, was a bad girl, a nasty girl, doing forbidden and nasty things.

Seventeen-year-old Barbara also recalled that next day small Barbara wandered dejectedly out onto the sidewalk, staring up the street for Daddy's car, when suddenly another fantasy struck her, as illogical as most fantasies are: *All of this is mother's fault.*

In blind rage Barbara lifted her doll. In fury she threw it down on the concrete. "I hate you. I hate you. You're dead. Dead. Dead."

For a moment she stared at the shattered pieces. Then picking them up she ran toward the house. As she rushed up the steps she stumbled and one of the sharp broken edges cut her arm.

That night Barbara did not suck her thumb. She was going to be a good girl. Then maybe Daddy and Mother would come back.

Toward morning she had her first attack of asthma.

"That was the start of it," Barbara now realized. She had had asthma ever since.

[46]

Subsequently Barbara talked more about this experience and came to understand it better along with other old, forgotten feelings. Belatedly she was able to bring the "bad" feelings out. And gradually her asthma disappeared.

"It's so easy," said Barbara in retrospect, "to hide things in illness and to disguise by boomeranging the suffering onto yourself that you wanted someone else to suffer.

"I see now that the doll was my mother. I see too that I tried to comfort myself with good body feelings. But when you've gotten the idea that bodies are bad and resentments are bad and you say to yourself, 'Poor me!' you're really saying, 'Bad me.' And you really don't like yourself at all."

THE TRUTH OF THE MATTER

And so it goes. All the hidings and denyings and disguises are promissory notes to peace of mind. But they are counterfeit. They leave the true feelings hidden and therefore less subject to guidance and rational control. They leave our children more frightened and more unhappy.

The same goes for us.

Without knowing why, countless adolescents—and countless adults—go through life not liking themselves and feeling wicked and bad.

Walling off the unwanted feelings from consciousness does not banish them.

UNCONSCIOUS FEELINGS
manage to
FIND THEIR OWN WAY OUT.

We do far better if we help our boys and girls see even belatedly that sex and body feelings are natural. So are resentments, with resentment to us, their parents, the most natural resentment of all.

[47]

5. In Guiding Your Teen-ager: Take First Things First

We have seen that hiding feelings is not effective. We've seen that feelings which remain hidden manage in some way to come out in uncontrolled and often in unhealthy, destructive and inappropriate acts.

To avoid the acts by which a teen-ager is apt to hurt himself and others, it is necessary for him to have the courage to *accept his own feelings* at the same time *maintaining his self-regard.* This you need to help him do. And this you can accomplish by letting him know that you accept his feelings—his "good" feelings and his so-called "bad" feelings—and that you think no less of *him.*

How important *acceptance* is, you yourself can testify if you stop to think.

WE ALL CRAVE ACCEPTANCE

When you have certain feelings and they're not understood, you feel disappointed and disapproved of. Your sense of intimacy and contact are broken.

"You're lucky that your child's accident wasn't worse!" This is mighty poor comfort when you've been worried over whether or not he would regain full motion in his fractured knee.

"It doesn't matter a bit that your cake fell; you'll do better next time!" This brings slim consolation. You care about *this* time; not next.

Father, trying to go against his own inner feelings and do what he believes he *ought* to do: "Cheer up, Son. What if you do have to miss playing in the final series game. By the time you're my age you won't remember."
Son, with anger joining his pain: "That's just the trouble with you. You don't remember!"

"You don't have to worry about that exam, Son. You know your stuff!" But this, too, does not help. It may instead estrange the son. He *is* worried and it's his *worry* that he wants you to understand.

Blond Ann looks up, her eyes blazing. "That mother of mine! She's got no more sense in her head than a flea. I tell her

I'm in love with Tom and she says, 'You'll get over it. You're only sixteen.' . . . As if my feelings didn't count simply because I'm two years underage. She makes me furious. I'd like to strike her dead. She doesn't understand me at all."

Young Pete, too, is angry. "You know what my dad said when I told him the other fellow got the job I'd been angling for? He said, 'Be sensible, Pete. There's no need for you to feel sore. Your boss never told you, did he, that he was going to give you that job?' Well, granted he hadn't. But it didn't make me feel any better to have my dad rub it in."

What Pete craved at the moment was not the sane, reasoning approach to disappointment. Nor was it a cheering-him-up kind of pity either that he craved. For this often carries a strange flat flavor.

"Don't feel bad, darling, that you lost your kitten! We'll get you another one tomorrow!" This cheers and consoles but it also directs the person away from his troubled feelings. And so it very subtly says, "You have no right to feel as you do."

"Don't worry, dear, over the operation. It isn't serious. Everything will be all right. It's done every day." Again the cheering on is present. But again the *true feelings are told to disappear.*

If someone implies that you should feel differently or tells you that you should not feel what you do feel, it doesn't make your feelings leave. The sense of disappointment or fear or chagrin or excitement is still in you. You can be told a dozen times, "Calm yourself now. Be steady!" But if you're not calm, such cautioning is obviously in vain.

> Telling a person
> NOT TO FEEL WHAT HE FEELS
> does NOT
> take the feelings
> AWAY.

Telling a person not to feel what he feels not only implies condemnation. It also forbids him to do something he can't help doing. He wants to stop. He can't. What you've done actually accentuates his feeling "bad." It is also apt to turn him against you.

When you feel that your husband or wife disregards your feelings, you tend to be disappointed and bitter. Your teenager is no different when you fail to take his feelings into account. He only grows more resentful and more antagonistic. Like Kim he may come to believe "It's no use listening to parents. They never listen to you."

> DISREGARDING
> your adolescent's
> TRUE FEELINGS
> makes
> him
> DISREGARD
> YOU.

What you crave and what he craves is understanding. Sympathetic understanding, we might call it, if by this term we mean the *acceptance of the feelings as they truly are*. Not glossing them over or prettying them, or trying to turn them, presto, into cheer.

What Pete wanted was to know that someone understood and accepted the soreness in him. "Trying for a job and then having it slide out from under your hands into someone else's —that does make you feel bitter!" It does.

What Ann wanted was someone to grant her the dignity and seriousness of feeling whatever she actually felt in her love for Tom. Had her mother just listened attentively, perhaps saying nothing but remembering back to her own teen-age moments of rapturous, sad and heart-searing romance, identifying and feeling *with* her daughter—then Ann would undoubtedly have felt her *with-ness*. And this would have helped Ann bring her true feelings into truer perspective. It would have carried her closer to bringing her actions under wiser control.

When you are upset or disturbed—whether it's because of a small disappointment like having a cake fall, or whether it's because of a large, frightening experience like an operation—what you want and need is to have someone *listen* and endure with you, *understanding how you really feel*.

The same is true of your adolescent.

> The EAR that ACCEPTS
> is a better
> FIRST
> than the tongue that
> suggests.

HELP HIM BRING OUT HIS FEELINGS

It helps a lot to face one's feelings and to bring them out into the open.

Then you're in a position to do more about them.

If they stay invisible, you are helpless.

It's been said: You can't mend a vase unless you see the pieces. Obviously—if the missing pieces are invisible you don't get very far.

Take young Jed. When Jed was a small child his father had been a traveling salesman, away from home a good part of the time. Jed had missed him. But Jed had also enjoyed having more of his mother in his father's absence. Most of all he'd enjoyed the coziness of sleeping in his father's bed. In his imagination he played he was Father, taking Father's place. And so, when his father got a new job that no longer took him away,

Jed was glad in a way, but mad also. In his mind he fantasied that his father was staying home purposely to punish him for having tried to take his place. But like the "good" little boy he was, Jed held the anger in. He shut it tightly down in his unconscious mind, where it remained hidden.

At seventeen, however, a curious thing was happening. Jed had one accident after another when he borrowed his father's car.

Junior's drive to beat the cop
Hides the wish to beat his pop.

His parents worried at first over his accidents and cheered him on to better driving. But when his mishaps continued, they condemned him for carelessness. They reasoned with him. They forbade him the use of the car for extended periods. But nothing worked.

"I don't know why I do it." Jed held his head in his hands. "Such stupidity! I let the car get going so fast I can't handle it. What happened last week was the final straw. I backed out of the driveway. I've backed out of it a millon times before. I know perfectly well that there's a lamppost right square across the street. But it was just as if I never knew the post was there. I went bang into it. And again I wrecked my father's car."

Jed couldn't help himself because he didn't see the feelings that were driving him.

However, after Jed had been helped by an acceptant person to *bring his true feelings* OUT he could acknowledge his anger toward his father. He could come to see finally that it had been groundless. And still more important, he saw that he had let his hostility come out in the act of wrecking his father's car.

Perhaps you've seen with your teen-ager just what Jed's parents noticed with him. That the techniques you've tried over the years don't work. This is because you have tried them without attending first to your young one's feelings. When you approach a problem without attending to feelings first, then—

> The reasoning technique does not work.
>
> The cheering technique does not work.
>
> The forbidding technique does not work.
>
> The condemning technique works least.

They all tell the troubled feelings to disappear. And this does no good.

Moreover they suggest dishonesty. They encourage a person to dissemble and hide what he feels.

But—after the feelings have been attended to, then it's different. Then focus can be put more profitably on behavior. With feelings out, the young person can pay more attention to how he should act.

Then—

> The reasoning technique often does work.
>
> The cheering technique often does work.
>
> The forbidding technique works too where it couldn't before.

[54]

The condemning technique even will work in its proper place.

In the past, we have been too prone to focus our attention on the troublesome behavior. We have left the troubled feelings to attend to themselves.

There's a better policy for us to adopt.

SEPARATE FEELINGS FROM ACTS

We need to distinguish between feelings and actions. They are not identical. Each needs its own type of treatment.

FEELINGS
always
NEED TO COME OUT;
ACTIONS
often
NEED HOLDING BACK.

In other words they need *opposite* handling, the one from the other. Whereas heretofore we have lumped them together and have tried to treat them both alike.

Out of this lack of separation many of our failures have grown.

We need to know securely that *feeling* a thing does not necessarily mean *doing* a thing.

FEELINGS ARE FACTS
but not necessarily
ACTS.

Certainly you feel bad when your cake doesn't rise in the baking. But that doesn't mean you have to smash the cake tin. Certainly Pete felt mad when his boss gave the coveted job to someone else. But that didn't mean he had to smash his boss.

[55]

Nor did Ann's saying that she wanted to strike her mother dead mean that she had to go ahead and do it.

You can want to buy a painting and yet not buy it. You can want to poison the neighbor for being nasty to your dog and yet never go near a pot of poison. You can feel at times like murdering your children and yet be a perfectly good parent. And so can they feel like murdering you.

Acknowledging the presence of an impulse does not mean that it must be carried out in an act that matches the impulse. *The better one can see what the impulse is, the better can one control the actions* toward which it pushes.

Young Jed had complained that the car had got going so fast he couldn't handle it.

What he'd implied was that his feelings had got going so fast he couldn't handle them.

Emotion is a powerful force that propels a person to do many untoward things. As we now know, many acts come from the push of feelings that are neither seen nor admitted. Since they are invisible to him, the person may, without even knowing it, let the feelings roll on and gather too much momentum to be comfortably steered. Then when he jams on the brakes, it does little good. He gets into trouble when he tries to maneuver a turn. However, if he first pays proper attention to cutting down the power, then the brakes do hold and he can turn safely into whatever road he chooses.

Just as with the force of the dashing car, so does the force of wild feelings need to be lessened. Then the actions which are geared to them can be more readily steered and controlled.

Facing the presence of the treacherous feelings is a desirable step. It can come best when the feelings have been accorded sufficient acceptance.

Then another step needs to be taken. The push of the feelings needs to be cut down.

[56]

In the talks Jed had with the counselor who accepted his feelings, he had been able to "spill" out again and again. He'd been able to bring out his anger, unreasonable though it was. Whether real or fancied, it had to travel along some outgoing path in order for him to do three things:

>to face his feelings
>>to reduce their force
>>>to control his behavior.

Father, who is still uninitiated: "Just look at that! He *feels* I'm a fool!"
Mother, who knows what's what: "But he *acts* as though you were a wise man far more since he's drawn how he feels."

Spilling briefly just once didn't do it. It seldom does. For the moment, perhaps. But, since the teen-ager's feelings have been long accumulating, they usually need more prolonged and repeated discharge.

LET HIM REDUCE THE PRESSURE INSIDE

Let's see how it works between parents and children.
Here is Rhea, fourteen, pinned to the TV, entranced with

the glamorous heroines she is secretly studying to emulate.

Then comes:

Scene as it was before Mother knew better

The time is after supper when Father wants to watch the wrestling matches. Rhea protests.

"Come on, now, Rhea," father growls, "it's my turn to have the show."

"You mean to *hog* the show," counters Rhea with an ugly leer.

"Here! Here, girl. Who's calling who what?"

"You said it," from nine-year-old Bud gleefully. *"She's* the pig."

"You scrub," mutters Rhea. "You just stay out of it . . ." And to Father, turning on her best wheedling, "Please, Dad, can't I have just a little more time?"

"Sorry," says Father, changing the channel as if Rome depended on it.

"You!" Rhea bursts out. "You! You old hypocrite. You're not really sorry at all."

"Why, Rhea." Mother scowls reproachfully while Father settles himself on the davenport. Bud wriggles down blissfully cherubic beside him, sucking at his bottle of Coke through a straw.

Rhea flounces out with looks that would kill if they could. She goes into the kitchen and starts stirring up some hot chocolate as a kind of soothing potion.

Mother just sits, knitting for dear life and gritting her teeth, when suddenly she hears a piercing shriek.

In the kitchen, Rhea is sobbing. She has spilled the boiling water from the kettle and has burned her leg.

That night there is no more wrestling match for Father and no more triumphant companionship for Bud.

Now let's turn the calendar forward and meet the family once more.

Scene sometime later after Mother had learned

Once more Rhea is watching her glamorous heroines. Once more Bud and Father come onto the scene.

"Okay, now, Rhea, now it's my time," from Father.

"But please, please, Daddy. Can't I ever have anything that *I* want?"

"Look, Rhea, it's my turn," from Father, decidedly.

And once again Rhea flounces out.

But this time, Mother rises and follows her down the hall.

"Come on into my room, Rhea. It's no fun, I know, feeling left out."

Rhea flops down on her mother's bed, her underlip curling, the tears welling up in her eyes. "Gee, Mom, I hate that goat-faced drag . . ."

Said Rhea's mother when she later related the incident, "I had it on the tip of my tongue to flare up, 'I won't have you talk about your father like that.' But I held my horses knowing the worst had to come out some way to reduce the pressure. And Rhea went on.

" 'That's all that Bud is. I can't stand his grin. What right has he to be so triumphant? He gets everything his way in this house . . .'

"My, was I glad I'd decided to listen. So here they were, Rhea's *real* feelings—anger at Bud for having her father. I remembered in a quick flash how I'd felt, the very same way only years and years back!

"I looked right at Rhea and, strangely, I didn't feel angry. I didn't feel like a stern taskmaster being called on to put her straight on the line. I felt *with* her, poor child! I realized she'd *acted* badly, but I realized, also, how important it was to pay attention to her feelings first. So I listened while she stormed. And she certainly did. Over and over: She hated Bud. She hated her father. I let her spill on and on. And then, all at once, with a great sob she gulped brokenhearted, 'They've got all those boy things to hold them together. Isn't Dad interested in girl things at all?'

" 'I know, dear,' I nodded, mirroring her feelings. 'You'd like Dad to have a little time just for you.'

"With that the sobs eased. 'Oh, Mom, you're so darling,' between moppings and sniffles. 'How did you ever get to understand?' "

So much for the moment. Rhea's mother knew there would be repetitions. There were bound to be. Meanwhile in this last scene several things had happened:

Rhea's *resentment had spilled out*.

It had been *met with sympathetic understanding*. Rhea's mother had communicated this to her daughter by putting what she sensed Rhea felt into *words that mirrored her feelings*. Rhea then knew she had a friend who didn't desert her out of believing as Rhea did about herself, that she was unworthy and greedy, unlikable and "bad."

Furthermore, having learned by listening how Rhea felt about her needs in relation to her father, Rhea's mother was in a position to tell him about this. As a result, some worthwhile steps could be taken to decrease Rhea's emotional hunger which not only was unnecessary but would also make resentment grow.

However, even before Rhea's mother had a chance to talk with Father, Rhea showed that her feelings were already somewhat changed. "How did you magic her?" he asked later that evening after Rhea had spilled. "When she kissed me good night she was actually *sweet*."

Her mother knew though that it wasn't magic. After the

outflow of the "bad" feelings and the sympathetic acceptance she had accorded them, good feelings came in.

After this, too, Rhea was more often willing to listen to reason she had always discarded before.

"Father works all day. At night he should have first choice of the TV! He needs to be considered, you know."

Mother, who has been to Psychology class that afternoon:
"Talk out your hates,
Don't drop the plates!"

At times Rhea assented. Since her feelings had been considered she was more willing to consider someone else's and comply in her acts.

At times she still protested. But with grievances coming repeatedly into the open, the fights over TV grew less intense. The flurries were over more quickly and the bitterness in them slackened.

Rhea had found she could share and bring out what she felt and have these feelings accepted. Although hanging onto the television could not be sanctioned, her feelings had not been condemned nor shut off.

[61]

Rhea's mother had MIRRORED them simply. And then she'd given them plenty of chance to SPILL OUT.

You can do the same.

LET HIM KNOW YOU UNDERSTAND

To do this—if you notice that your son or your daughter is bewildered, sore or disgruntled—open it up—don't pass it over. Watch carefully. Listen attentively. Try to see how your youngster feels. And say what you observe aloud in order to communicate that you are acceptant and willing to have him bring out more of his feelings.

"You look bothered, Sis!" Or "I know, Bud, this surely must make you mad!"

Try to
GET THE FEEL OF WHAT HE'S FEELING
and try to
MIRROR HIS FEELINGS WITH YOUR WORDS.

You may need to introduce your new policy with a news-flash. "I've got some sense at last about this business of feelings. I read a book which explained that it only makes matters worse to hold feelings in. So let's start a new program. If you feel mad, you tell me . . ."

"And if you're mad?" ,

"I'll tell you, too."

"That's not new."

"No. But from your side it will be. We've never before tolerated your griping. We've sat on you. Remember? We've said, 'Look here, you don't appreciate how good you have it.' Or we've told you that you shouldn't complain. Or we've scolded, 'You shouldn't talk that way to your mother.' Or we've insisted, 'You don't *really* feel that way,' when you actually did.

"But now we know better. And we've a hunch that after

[62]

you've brought out your grievances for a while in big doses, you won't need to get mad as often or as much. Anyway, let's give it a try."

Sometimes no matter what we do, it doesn't help. No matter how many "horrible" feelings we listen to, a child's problems go on. There are a number of reasons for this. Chief among these is the fact that he may be "spilling" about the *feelings that* HIDE his true feelings and NOT about the real feelings that are troubling him. Mona, for instance, weeps and complains that she feels so shy; that she doesn't dare talk to anybody; that everyone knows so much more than she, and that they don't like her. What is actually bothering her, however, is the anger against a more brilliant sister which she is covering up. Her timidity is a denial of how she really feels.

As parents (or teachers) we cannot and should not prod for these undercover feelings. We can only give opportunity to let come what comes.

Sometimes as we *remain* acceptant the child of his own accord moves on and brings out more of the hidden feelings. Sometimes, if there are problems that keep on disturbing him and us—we are wise to seek professional help, realizing that the trained person is better equipped to get at the undercover, hidden feelings which are causing the problems to go on.

In any case it may happen when you start to mirror "mean" feelings that your youngster very positively denies what you say. "No," he may avow with a mean look in his eye, "I don't feel mean at all." Or, instead of frank denial, he may put on a saintly, I'm-better-than-you sort of air.

Many times this is no more than a passing defense against admitting feelings he has long believed he had to deny. If it happens, don't be insistent! Don't push him to admit these particular feelings at this particular time. But persist in showing *your* acceptance of them as other occasions arise.

[63]

At this point, it may be wise to stop and ask yourself some questions.

Are you still afraid that if you let a child of yours "go on" about such feelings they will increase?

Are you still afraid that if he brings such feelings out, he will have to carry them over into action?

You've heard now that neither of these things need happen. But, after all, you have heard the other side for many long years.

Haven't you been taught all your life that unpretty feelings are unacceptable? Weren't you taught very early specifically that hostile feelings and sex feelings in a child were especially unthinkable?

You can't expect yourself to get over your old feelings all at once. You'll probably wander back and forth between the old and the new many times.

You may hate to think, for instance, that any child of yours could have hidden resentment to a new baby beneath the sweetness he showed. One part of you protests. Another part says, "Yes, I feel that was true." And this part feels also that there was resentment aplenty to the new baby's mother. As one child put it, "She shouldn't have brought so much bother home from the hospital."

One part of you protests against the idea that your teen-agers literally hate you at moments. Another part of you knows full well that this also happens.

One part of you blames yourself for it. Another part wisely counters that when your teen-agers were small you didn't know how to help them handle their feelings. It was natural, as a result, that anger against both the actual and fantasied "wrongs" should have piled up.

One part of you is still afraid to see these things come out

[64]

into the open. The other part of you has courage enough to say, "Go ahead."

It's natural for resentment and anger to enter afresh into close relationships as life moves on. There are bound to be loving and hostile moments both between sisters and brothers, between husbands and wives, between parents and children.

Both
HOSTILITY AND LOVE
are bound to exist
IN EVERY CLOSE RELATIONSHIP.

Hostility does not ordinarily exclude love.

But—

Hostility can become dangerous and choke out love when it is shoved down into the unconscious and is left there indefinitely to spread.

However, it is not safe for hostility to come out willy-nilly. Of this you can be justifiably afraid.

HE STILL NEEDS YOU

Getting rid of "bad" feelings any old way does not help.

Suppose a boy holds up a bank, taking the clerk as a symbol of his father, just as Jed took the car as a symbol. Obviously bringing out his hostility in this manner can only make his fears and his troubles increase. Besides worse things happening, he accumulates other father symbols to fear and hate— namely, the police.

On the other hand, if a child broods alone in solitary fashion over his hurts either real or imagined, he consciously or unconsciously builds up fantasies of what he would like to do to get even and he frightens himself. Then what usually happens is that he is taken to task by the policeman part of himself

[65]

which he long ago acquired by being father-inside-himself to himself. He may become painfully severe with himself, driving himself into depressed helplessness for one thing, afraid of venturing anything lest he venture too much. Or he may become an ascetic, punishing himself out of enjoyment, becoming prudish and prissy and over good.

Let us repeat: Getting "bad" feelings out any old way does not help. It does not help to get them out in dangerous pursuits or in solitary imaginings. Neither does it help to have them accepted, say, by some fellow "delinquent" whom one doesn't respect. Nor by a friend, even, of one's own age who one feels is basically no stronger than oneself.

Troubled feelings must be got out to a person from whom the teen-ager can gather strength. This means YOU or another acceptant adult.

They must be got out in acts that do not get him into trouble.

They must be got out in ways that let him rest in the firm knowledge that he has done no actual harm.

And they must, as you know, be got out in ways that do not shatter self-regard . . .

When enough
"BAD" FEELINGS HAVE COME OUT
in ways that
lessen fear
and that
safeguard the adolescent's feelings of his own worth
—then—
GOOD FEELINGS FLOW IN.

It's as if getting out the "bad" feelings had made more room for love to enter so that our youngster is more richly equipped to fight the good fight from within.

6. He Doesn't Have to Obey That Impulse

CONTROL IS A MUST

'Way back when he was little, this teen-ager of yours may have wakened from sleep at night, startled by dreams that brought from his unconscious mind impulses so terrifying that they made him cry out. A dream of choking baby sister, for instance, may have come too close to a conscious wish. In any case, he had the impulse to do many frightening things. But his littleness in a way was a guarantee of safety. He knew that you would stop him and that you *could* because you were big.

But now in his new bigness, you may be no bigger than he. His body has grown to such size and strength that should he let himself go, he fears he may run amok. And so, to feel safe, he needs to know very firmly from you that controls are a *must*.

By now we have seen that we cannot dictate to him how he should feel or how he should not feel. Neither can he dictate this to himself. We cannot change his feelings by telling him to feel one way and not to feel another. Neither can he change his own feelings by telling himself to change them. He feels what he feels and that is that.

As we've seen, he can, however, sometimes come to feel differently as he faces his feelings and gets them off his chest in ways *that essentially preserve his sense of integrity and self-respect.*

To this end—

> There can be no restrictions on how he feels. On the other hand, there must be restrictions on how he acts.

To acquire control he must learn:

> To recognize how he feels;
> To express his feelings as they are and for what they are
> But—
>
>> To express them only *in certain* WAYS
>>   *at certain* TIMES
>>   and
>>   *in certain* PLACES.

"We've begun to see that griping is important, Jim. And we want to hear how you feel. But we will not tolerate your showing your resentment by slamming doors when your great Aunt Patricia's here! There's a better way of doing it and a better time and place."

Your teen-ager wants to know that his feelings are natural, not monstrous, so that he may know he is not monstrous in having them. Furthermore, he wants to learn how to handle his feelings as much as you want him to. He wants to find that he doesn't have to obey that impulse. That there are things he can do to bring it more readily under control.

How to help him, that's still the big question—*to bring out his feelings freely, honestly and safely in acts he* CONTROLS.

"Gee, you're swell," says Johnny to his father who has found how to do it. "You 'most always understand that I simply gotta feel the way I feel I gotta. But, when it's important, you see to it that I gotta *do* as I should."

We gripe. We voice grievances. Complain. Revile and swear. All these are ways in which we commonly let out negative feelings through the spoken word.

We can also use the written word as outlet. Common instances of this range from belligerent editorials and smear campaigns to poison-pen letters and pornographic scribblings on lavatory walls.

With pencil and brush still other outlets come into play. The bitter political cartoon is just one example.

The persons who take these outlets may be justifiably angry at the targets against which they strike. On the other hand they may be venting only feelings that cover the real source of their anger. Or their shame may mount with what they are doing so that the letting out fails to bring relief.

In schools and in youth groups of one sort or another, drawing, painting, modeling, writing and dramatics have all been used successfully as action channels through which troubled feelings may flow.* Sometimes and with some teen-agers these activities have also been used in the home.

Thirteen-year-old Larry, for instance, draws cartoons. In his comic strip he has two characters. He calls them Big Gnash and Little Gnash, and the latter invariably triumphs over his larger counterpart. In this fashion, Larry, with his pencil, battles with his father, who accepts it good-naturedly.

"So," he says, "I see! The kid here in your strip is taking his father's car on the sly. Pretty tricky. All kids would like to get by with things like that. Me, too. I used to want to . . ."

"Like me right now," grins Larry. "I'd like to, sure. But I know I can't."

(Notice particularly that Larry's father did not go into a lecture on the morals or ethics attached to car stealing. Even

* See Chapter 14.

if Larry had not said so, he would have known that Larry already knew full well what constituted the rights and the wrongs in such a situation.)

Larry's father remembered hearing that the nagging irksomeness of countless forbiddings defeats their purpose. As another youngster put it, "It makes me heedless when you needle me with so many needless things."

Sometimes through games such as tennis or golf or checkers or chess, members of the family can fight out battles, and if some of the usual emphasis on good sportsmanship is waived, they can even own up to the enmity that accompanies the shots and the moves.

For some teen-agers, activities such as these are more effective pathways to follow than talk of and by itself.

All in all, however, the most direct way for adolescents (and for adults too, for that matter) is to get feelings out through the channel of talk.

THE DIFFICULT MOMENTS
AND THE "DO'S" AND THE "DONT'S"

We know, and we will reiterate, some things can't be done because of health and safety. Some things cannot be permitted because property must be protected. Some things are important because of law and order, some because of ethical considerations, moral and religious ideologies and because of social codes. And some things we cannot tolerate because they go against us and what we believe and are.

Sometimes, for reasons of our own—or our family's—we want or don't want things done. As we've seen we have a right to our own feelings too.

"No. The radio can't be on now. Dad's got the income tax to do and the music disturbs him."

"I'm not willing to tidy up after you as though you were five. You're not. If you have the privilege of pulling ginger ale

[70]

bottles out of the refrigerator, you also have the responsibility of cleaning up."

However, we need also to grant our boy or girl the right to express how he honestly feels in response to such demands. And we can be very sure that he *will* feel mean and resentful at times. It's in the cards. If he doesn't, he isn't natural. So why not relax and expect him to grumble back at us? Then we won't have to feel so indignant when he does. Gone are the days, or so we hope, when our children are so fearful or so hypocritical that they do with amiable purrs what they hate doing.

"I know you don't like to do this. I know you resent it. You can call me names under your breath or out loud. But," turning back to what is required, "it's still got to be done."

This doesn't mean that name calling or other showings of "meanness" need to be tolerated at all times. Certainly not when Mother is due to take a cake from the oven or when guests are present. "Hold it, Ginny," says Ginny's mother brusquely. "We'll take it up later after Grandmother's gone."

And this leads us into ACTION PLANNING as part of the teenager's life. What to DO when flurries and scurries arise? And WHAT NOT TO DO? Both need definition.

Make it clear, as we have already indicated, that when hostile feelings arise certain things can be done and certain things cannot be done about them.

"You can paint it out. Play it out. Dance it out. Moan it out. Talk it out. But no pummeling. No kicking the door like a four-year-old. No running away to make me sorry. No shouting of swear words out in the yard where the whole neighborhood can hear."

These are policies concerning actions in general. There can also be *action planning* to cover certain types of situations that repeatedly arise.

Betsy and Joe are continuously at each other and now once

more Betsy is shrieking in a voice that can be heard down several city blocks, not alone in the apartments on either side and above and below. "You cur. You touched my uke. I can tell you touched it. You fat-headed pig."

"Stop it, Betsy," Father growls. "Stop shouting and stop it right now. I've told you one million times that even if you don't, *I* do care what the neighbors think."

But Betsy goes merrily on.

Father menacingly rolls up his paper while Betsy, cringing down in her chair, bursts into loud sobs and glowers at Joe, who gloats with triumph.

And just at this moment Mother walks in.

"Hold everything," Mother commands. Her voice is fresh with inspiration. She has just heard a talk and the Word is in her: "Feelings come first."

Since Betsy obviously is the most bothered, she starts with her. "You're furious at Joe, aren't you, Betsy?"

Betsy's jaw drops. This is new business. She gulps and she nods, suddenly quiet. (Her feelings have been taken into account.)

"And you're mad at Betsy, Jim, I know, for making so much noise." Mother goes over and kisses Father and gives him a little reassuring pat. "And as for you, Joe," turning to Brother, "you look happy as a fox. Triumphant, I'd call it, and sort of wicked. I'll bet you're glad you started the hubbub."

All three stare dumfounded. This is quite different from Mother's usual hair-tearing act.

Mother turns again to Betsy. Yes, she observes, Betsy is still the most upset. "Here, Betsy," she says aloud, reaching into the desk for pencil and paper, "I'll tell you what. When people get mad, they *want* to do mean things. Here, draw a picture, just a quick sketch of what you'd like to do to Joe." (Mother is suggesting an action pathway along which Betsy may let her feelings come out.)

[72]

Something sure and consenting in Mother's tone opens the gateway and Betsy draws swiftly: a sketch of herself with a gun, shooting her brother.

"I know," nods Mother, "you'd like to shoot him. Daddy really knows too. Sometimes he'd like to do the same thing to me."

"Why, Edith!" gasps Father. "Have you gone crazy?"

"No, dear, not quite!" And Mother explains what it's all about. "And now, for a little action planning. Next time, Betsy, when you feel mean to Joe, draw out how you feel. Don't yell it out. The yelling only makes your father mad and makes things worse for you." (Some action channels are better than others.)

"And as for you, Joe, when you get annoyed with Betsy as I know you frequently do, what will you plan to do?"

"Kick her in the shins!"

"No soap." (Limiting the actions.)

"Pull her ears."

"No go, either. Why not try a limerick of what you'd like to do to her?" (This action pathway is okay.)

"Aw shucks, Mother, that's no fun."

However, after dinner at the usual high peak of the evening bickers, all is curiously still. Then Betsy appears with another picture, and beside her is Joe. Quickly he thrusts his paper under Mother's nose. On it she reads:

> There was a young silly from Sioux
> Who was stinky as any old shoe.
> When she opened her trap
> She did nothing but yap.
> I'd like to plaster her mouth shut with glue.

"Nice business," mutters Father.

But an hour later, he comes from the study and smiles broadly at Mother. "By golly, it works. They've got the radio on together in mutual agreement for the first time in their lives."

So far we've dealt mostly with the handling of hostile feelings—one of the roots of trouble in adolescence. Later in the book we shall focus on matters of sex. Suffice it to say here that these too need to be talked through in terms of how feelings can legitimately be handled, taking into consideration the individual's development, circumstances, ideals and time of life.*

What to do, too, about the dozen and one specific things, sex-tinged, that come up in adolescence? And what not to do? Always, however, allowing outlets for the feelings of resentment that are bound to happen when restrictions must be met. About Judy's neckline, for instance, on the black velvet bodice.

"You look beautiful, Judy, with that off-shoulder business!" from Father. "But," with a skeptical raising of brows, "isn't it too low in front?"

"But Dad, I look nice, don't I?"

"Yes, dear, terrific. In fact, too bewitching."

"You mean you won't let me wear it?"

"You want to, I know." (Acknowledging feelings.)

"Yes, Dad, I sure do. It's natural, isn't it, to like being attractive?" Judy's voice rose into shrillness.

"Quite natural. And it's natural too, Judy, to get angry when you feel someone's stymieing you."

"Oh, darn! You old dodo. You're sixty years behind the times." And Judy raved on.

Father listened, knowing that all children think their parents old-fashioned and that they need to get these feelings off their chests.

* See Chapters 7 through 10.

Finally Judy stopped belaboring her father and with hands on hips, glaring at him, asked, "Well, what am I supposed to do?"

(With those feelings out, thought Father, we're more ready to meet the situation.) "How about it?" He looked Judy over once more. "Why not get Mother to put some hems around the neck somewhere to raise it just enough?"

"Oh, Daddy, you old nut. *Darts,* you mean!" And Judy spun around, laughing, and with a swift peck on the top of Father's head she threw out a parting, good-natured jibe. "Okay, old man, have it your way."

With your particular youngster, you will feel some things important to insist on and some things not.

At certain moments, too, it will be wiser not to insist on the very same things you have insisted on at other moments. The adamant, consistent rule of once-for-all-time is not the order of the day. It's better to consider the time, his time, your time right now.

Every so often you may still feel a need to fall back on long-used punishments such as reduction of privileges following shirking of responsibilities. But you will find that such measures become much less necessary after you have given, and continue to give, plenty of opportunity to let the troublesome feelings come out more directly.

Two other things will also make a great difference in reducing the difficult moments.

If a teen-ager has enough really good and vital emotional satisfactions, he won't as often become as troubled or as troublesome. When his emotional needs and hungers and drives are properly fulfilled, then his problems do actually diminish. We shall, therefore, want to check and *see that he does achieve*

[75]

the satisfactions he is after in so far as the strivings that drive him are compatible with the circumstances in which he lives and with his ideals for himself and ours for him.

That's one thing. The other is this:

If we guard against too many demands and curbings, he will comply more readily with those which we do impose. It helps a lot to cut down on the *requests that are relatively unimportant*. For all of us know that a heap of curtailments and expectations that seem unjustified cause resentment to rise at any age. They bring rebellion in their wake and make control more difficult.

Putting these two over-all principles more concisely: We will keep in mind steadfastly that EMOTIONAL SATISFACTIONS NEED TO BE STEPPED UP AS MUCH AS IS POSSIBLE and that DEMANDS AND FORBIDDINGS NEED TO BE STEPPED DOWN AS MUCH AS IS PRACTICAL.

Nor will we forget that our children will be far more reasonable about our reasonable requests if we show them that we can, at least sometimes, accept their feelings whether or not these seem reasonable to us at all times.

THE SECOND CHANCE YOU'VE ALWAYS WANTED

"If I could only live my life over, I'd do things very differently for my children during their first few years. I made too many mistakes."

How many of us feel similarly! How many of us wish we might go back and have a second chance!

Actually, a child's adolescence brings with it this second chance. It's been said that adolescence is emotionally like a second infancy and early childhood. In this period of heightened growth, as we have already recognized, the youth recapitulates many of the feelings that he had during his first earlier period of rapid growth. Many of the yearnings and conflicts kindled then are rekindled now.

[76]

And so, as you recognize and understand and accept the feelings that he has now about current things, you are in effect accepting past attitudes that are rolled up in these current feelings.

You can in addition do something more direct.

DON'T LET BYGONES BE GONE

The teen-ager has many realistic current grievances. He meets up with cliques or gangs and is excluded, for instance. His anger at those who snub him is realistically directed at them. But if he pins on his dentist the picture of a bad man who purposely is out to hurt him, not only is this unrealistic but it leads him into feeling greater fear than is warranted and greater dislike of the dentist.

When his turmoil seems out of proportion to the actual person or event that he blames for it, one very important point to remember is that, in many instances, the roots of his exaggerations reach back into childhood to where his feelings and fantasies were centered on us, his parents. As we've seen, it is this very reaching back that often makes him overly angry at us now and makes his anger also spread out onto others. It is this same reaching back that makes him offer us those exaggerated objections he so often gives.

"But when things are past," you may still ask, "what can we do about them now? Isn't it best to let bygones be bygones?"

It isn't. When bygones stay hidden the troubles they contain grow larger.

Instead of letting bygone sore feelings stay hidden a better policy is to help your teen-ager gripe belatedly about the objections and "bad" feelings he used to have.

Because of your new insights and your new ability to accept many of his feelings, you'll do better with his old feelings now than you did then. He'll have a chance to relive them, as it were, with a more understanding parent than he had then.

[77]

And this, in turn, can help him rid himself of some of their pressure and show him belatedly that he isn't so bad as he felt he was.

Charles's father recounts, "We have what we call REMEMBERING TIMES. They aren't set programmed moments. They can come in at any hour of the day.

"The other evening Charles got peeved about something inconsequential. Anyway, he looked at me with utter scorn and called me a dope.

"I let him rave and a little later I said, 'Remember, Charles, when you were a kid, one afternoon you called me some name and I let you have it across the mouth?'

" 'You bet I do,' ruefully. 'Gee, I hated you. Let's face it, Pop, that was a horrible thing for a big man to do to a little boy. I never wanted to exterminate anybody so much in my life!'

" 'Check!' I said. 'It was rotten of me.'

" 'Uh-huh,' he came back. 'That was before you had any sense.' "

Noreen's mother brought past things up in similar manner with Noreen.

"Remember how I used to punish you?"

"Oh, Mom! The worst thing was the eating business. Remember the way you used to make me sit and sit. For hours. I'll never do anything like that to a child of mine. It makes you want to throw up all over everything . . ."

"And everybody?"

"You said it. And especially over one person."

"I can guess who that was."

It's a fallacy for us older ones to think, "You young squirt, you've got your whole life ahead of you!"

He hasn't. He, too, has a past. He has a history of past occurrences and wants. He also has a history of past feelings.

It's true, as far as the occurrences and events are concerned, that what's past is past. You can't undo it. It's done.

Fortunately, feelings are more malleable. You can make up for past mistakes by present acceptance. Going back into past feelings and bringing them out can sometimes also bring a fresh start.

TO LESSEN
"BAD" FEELINGS stored up from TIMES PAST
reminisce and
BRING THEM OUT
NOW.

The most important part of this whole matter of helping present-tense feelings hitch up with past grievances is to get the focus off substitute oppressors back onto the original oppressors—namely, us.

Ted's mother listened to Ted's complaints about his teacher. "You make her sound as bad as you used to think me."

This started the ball in her own direction and put the focus back onto her.

Molly's mother noticed that Molly had been irritable and irritated with the housekeeper. And so while she and Molly were doing the mending together one day she remarked, "You get as mad at Maggie as you used to at me."

Molly jumped in, "That's right, Ma, let's face it. You're getting less fussy in your old age, but you used to be an awful bag." And Molly ranted on.

"I didn't push or insist," Molly's mother said in recounting the incident. "I just offered Molly the opportunity. I thought if she did happen to feel that *I* was the villain behind the scenes it would give her a chance to pick it up . . . After she yipped at me she seemed to see Maggie in truer perspective. She stopped splashing her feelings from me onto her."

[79]

Both Ted's and Molly's mothers were helping their youngsters direct their feelings back onto the targets from which they had been displaced.

YOUR PLATFORM IN BRIEF

Perhaps at this point you are clamoring: "Some specific directions, please!"

By now no doubt you've got the gist of what *you'd* like to do. If so, you'll be able to fill in the following short sentences with your own expanded meanings.

Keep the ear in tune and the eyes open.

Take stock of what your teen-ager seems to be wanting.

Supply whatever emotional hungers you can.

Pick up his present-tense feelings when they are troubled and help him get them off his chest.

To start him off, try mirroring them with your words.

Give him a chance to get back at you now for the past feelings that may still lie in the way of friendship between you.

Remain as sympathetically acceptant as you can of his FEELINGS.

Deal firmly and realistically with controls that are needed concerning his ACTS.

THE FEEL-HOW IS PART OF IT

"All of this is very fine! But isn't it a little too much to expect us parents to keep up sympathetic understanding when we find ourselves bearing the brunt of most of our children's gripings?"

"How can we be expected never to get insulted or mad?"
You're not.

You're bound to get mad at times. You're bound to get insulted at times. You're bound to get angry at times. And if you do, it's better to show it than to act one way while feeling another.

Parents have feelings too!

If you try out your new-learned "acceptance" business feeling artificially sweet, it will never work.

"My mother," says one girl, "she never hollers. She smiles. But her hollerings are stamped all over her face."

"My father," says another, "it would be better if he cussed out loud rather than to himself. He acts all controlled and quiet. But he makes me feel he's hating me inside."

"My mom's gotten this new technique," confides another. "She's supposed to mirror your feelings. I looked in the book. So she says sweetly, 'You're feeling angry!' But I know mighty well that underneath she's muttering to herself, 'You're a brat!' "

It doesn't work to accept with words and reject underneath. Better to let your own anger out and later, if you really feel like going back over what's happened, to approach it with sincere humility or contrition or belated sympathy or whatever it is that you do *honestly* feel.

"I got mad. But now that that's over, I do see how you were feeling. I'm mad at myself that I had to explode."

Ask yourself:

When I'm angry, am I ashamed to show it?

Am I perhaps steering away from letting my children show anger because I'm afraid of angry feelings in myself?

Does it make sense to me, the whole idea of letting these children of mine come out with their troubled feelings—not here, there and everywhere, but alone in the intimate course of our living together?

Am I still afraid that they may get the habit of splashing out at everyone if I let them splash out at us? Or can I see that rather the reverse is true—that they actually splash less at others when they have chances to get out their feelings at us? And in the end they have more room for love!

Do I, by now, sense the hang of it?

Am I ready to learn how to do it?

If you feel you are ready, there's only one way really to learn how: that's to TRY.

PART TWO: THEY CRAVE A NEW DEAL IN SEX EDUCATION

7. What Every Teen-ager
Wants to Know

Bess, small-boned and dark and trimly sixteen, covered her face with her hands and sobbed, "I wish so terribly I hadn't done it! Why didn't anyone tell me the truth?"

Bit by bit her story unrolled. She'd been a lonely little girl, her father preoccupied with his business, her mother a conscientious woman lacking in warmth. Keith, her boy friend, was two years older, a head taller, studious, earnest and industrious too. In vacations he'd worked as a machinist and had managed to put several hundred dollars aside.

For a month of nights they had lain together on the warm sand in a little cove they had discovered and played was their home. To Bess it had felt immeasurably good, with a "comforting kind of goodness more than a sexy one."

"Keith was told by some of the fellows that if you took certain precautions nothing would happen." Only something had happened. Even though Keith had been ever so careful.

They were frantic. Keith had finally found out what to do. White-faced and with set mouth, he took Bess to a street corner one morning where, according to instructions, he left her to wait alone for the car that would pick her up.

Anxious, he huddled behind a nearby junk heap so that his nearness might bring her more courage.

[85]

Then the car had come with the man and the other girls. Five of them, jammed in. And they had driven across the border into a small gambling town to a dirty gray building where unspeakable fear had gripped her. The rumpled sheet on the operating table. The dirty looking hands of the doctor . . .

"Keith and I love each other and we want to get married as soon as we're old enough. But the memory of something like this twists in between us . . .

"We didn't know you could get pregnant that way. Our folks never told either of us much . . . My mother tried to give me the facts of life. But she left out the things I wanted most to talk about. She was afraid I'd go too far if I knew too much. But I think you go further when you don't know enough . . ."

Keith and Bess were not "bad." They were bewildered. Their questions about sex had never really been answered. Not because their parents hadn't tried. But because their parents hadn't known.

As one sees a goodly number of teen-agers and listens to their questions and wonderings, certain points emerge. In spite of the thought and time that many of us, as parents, have put into the matter of providing our children with sex education, they still go unsatisfied. Something is missing. Like Bess, they keep wondering and seeking, they know not what.

By taking into account what these teen-agers say, we become aware of omissions they would like to have mended, of areas they would like to have expanded, of emphases they would like to have brought out.

We discover that they are seeking something that we have not even thought of as a part of sex education.

Implicit in what they ask and tell us lie complaints that point to new directions they hope we will take.

[86]

The teen-ager does not want *the* facts of life. He wants *his* facts of life. Not facts looking back in reference to when he was born, but facts about the present and facts looking forward to when he will have love and marriage and children of his own.

"I want to know about me now and me in the future," says Bill, eager and honest. "And I want those left-out parts put in with plenty of details to make them plain."

Both boys and girls want to know about their own bodies and those of the opposite sex. About shape and form; about the changes that occur during adolescence; about what happens outside, and also inside, of the body out of sight:

"I'm terrible, I know," a thirteen-year-old girl confides. "But I'd like to see what a boy really looks like without bathing trunks or anything else on. I try to see when the water's gotten the outline to show, but I get to feeling too ashamed. Do you think you could draw it or show me a picture without any old fig leaf on?"

About menstruation: From thirteen-year-old Tony, "Just what happens to girls in certain parts of the month? My sister gets something wrong with her. When I asked about it, she said she had the curse. When I asked what that was she said, 'Shut up.'"

Tony was very serious. His knotted scowl betrayed apprehension. "Is it catching? Won't you please tell me something to make it more clear?"

From a girl not quite thirteen, "I know about ministration. That's what happens to women. Now I'd like to know about menstration or whatever it is that happens to men."

About seminal emissions, many a boy asks: "Are wet dreams normal?" with anxiety showing . . . "How often do you get

[87]

them? If I lose too much will I get old while I'm young?"

About bodies in the grip of labor and birth: "Just where does the baby come out of?" with curiosity less evident than fear. "Is there really a big enough hole?" . . . And from a boy whose concern is of more practical nature, "Is there something particular you do to make a girl have twins or thripples? I simply gotta know so I can stay away from it. I plan to be a veterinary and they don't get rich quick. So one baby at a time's going to be enough for me."

Most tremendously important to both boys and girls are *questions about making love and mating.*

With the plea for details again apparent, "How often?" . . . "How?" . . . "When?" . . . And, once more with a note of fear entering, "Do you lose your strength from it?"

But most frequently, with variations, over and over, "How does it feel?"

HOW ABOUT THE SURGES AND URGES?

These teen-agers don't want us to stop with attention to facts. Their quest goes further. It has to do with feelings as well. Especially the swift surge of body feelings that flood through them. This is concern number one.

"Do girls have the same sexy feelings that boys have?" . . . "Do your own thrills run into a girl when you hold her hand?" . . . "Is it normal to feel those ruffles down your back?" . . . "What on earth do they do at nudist camps where they can't hide anything? Or is it more legal for nudists to feel the way they do than it is for us?"

"Why are thoughts more forceful than a cold shower? You take the shower to take away the thoughts but it does no good. Am I a sex maniac, do you suppose?"

"When I look at those big boys in the senior class with their broad shoulders and all, they look so beautiful I melt. I get all goose-pimply and I wonder if I'm one of those terrible nymphs or whatever they call it."

The more they talk, the more apparent it becomes that these boys and girls have a great deal of anxiety tied up with their body feelings. They may act wise and knowing. But underneath they are uncertain and tense.

Ted is fifteen, on the short side, a shy boy, having difficulty in concentrating on school subjects. His teachers report that he is often off in the clouds and that he has an anxious, tense look.

Yes, he is worried, he confides to the psychologist. He is worried about his size. He'd grown some, but would he ever grow big enough? Lots of the fellows were bigger. Especially in certain parts.

Then, reddening up to the roots of his hair, he voiced a question that had long been troubling him. "Can you get yourself stunted by things you've done that are 'bad'?"

Long ago he'd had sex play with some neighborhood children, furtively and with fear of discovery, until one day he was found and beaten. And now when he looked at a pretty girl, the same sort of body feelings surged through him. They reminded him of his earlier "badness" and they brought in anew the old fears.

It so happened that Ted's parents had answered his questions quite factually. But *they had never answered his worries*.

In consequence, they had left out of his sex education what he was most desperately seeking—*surcease from pain*.

EASING the teen-ager's ANXIETIES
ABOUT BODY FEELINGS
is a most important part of the sex education
he craves.

[89]

Many times instead of helping reduce a youngster's anxiety, we unwittingly augment it by dire warnings against disease.

Seventeen-year-old Laura shied away from contacts with boys. Her ardent nature, her parents feared, was leading her into a too close and intimate friendship with another girl. As Laura unloaded her worries to the psychologist to whom they took her, it became clear that the immediate thing contributing to her avoidance of men was her fear of disease.

"You can't tell whether or not a man has got it! And you can get it even by kissing! I'm scared."

Other boys and girls express similar anxiety in their questions: "Can you get the sex disease when you come too close and get the breathing in your face like with colds?" . . . "Can you ever get cured once you've had it? Some say there are drugs. Some say it keeps coming back so your children turn into idiots." . . . "They showed us pictures. Sores and things. I've got a bad skin. Do you think I could have caught it without knowing?"

Some show their fear openly. Some pass it off with bravado. "I'm not scared. I can get by all right. I've managed with a lot of girls and have never caught anything," Rog declared. But night after night he woke from sleep groaning, startled out of dreams in which his body had been woefully maimed.

As Laura went on exploring her feelings more deeply, she discovered that her anxiety had not started with the recent fear of disease. It had started much further back with the sex thoughts and feelings she had had as a child. The more recent warnings against disease had tuned in with a familiar chord of earlier warnings and set off old fears in new settings.

In most instances, what the teen-ager hears today forms bridges across time to many things in his past. Common among these is what happened to him when he found that by touching himself he could produce pleasurable sensations.

Ordinarily when a child does this, if it is discovered, his parents show dismay, or worse.

One intelligent girl relates, "When I was about six my mother came in and discovered me touching myself. She hissed through her teeth 'Pig' and went out with the most scathing coldness. Her rejection, I think, was worse than any more violent threat."

Even when parents have heard through lectures and reading that masturbation is not harmful, they may, because of their own backgrounds, still feel revulsion. Valiantly though they may have tried to hide it, their child has undoubtedly sensed this. For children have uncannily acute feelers which they seem to keep alerted to the inner thoughts and emotions of the adults on whom they depend.

In instances where actual threats have been nonexistent, the child often fills in the gaps with his imagination. "When you are bad," he has learned, "you must expect to be punished." He has applied this, unwittingly, to the matter at hand. "If your body is bad," his fantasy has said in effect, "then your body will suffer. Punishment is sure to come. And what punishment could be worse than being crippled or hurt?"

Some boys and quite a few girls neither recognize nor remember this. They have forgotten the frightening threat or the tightened voice or the raising of brows. They have forgotten the act itself, and their fantasies about it. But in their unconscious minds, traces remain of fear and of the sense of being "bad." Other boys and girls remember. In either case, both actual and imagined threats still exert their influence. The questions these youths ask betray their apprehension.

"Does it make you shrink and get smaller?"

"Does it get you so weak that you have to wear a brace?"

"Does it hurt you so that you can never have babies?" with a plea for relief behind the worried look.

Nineteen-year-old Caroline has been married six months and is struggling between her frigidity and her wish to enjoy herself vividly. She had been told as a child that she was bad to touch herself and that it might injure her so that she would never enjoy intercourse.

"They kept impressing on me to keep down the sex feelings. But now, all of a sudden, I'm told those very same feelings won't hurt me and I'm expected to turn on the switch."

She had been worried that she might injure herself. She had been told she was nasty. So now, underneath her wholesome wish to react to her husband with vigor and warmth, Caroline still felt fear and self-condemnation. It was only after she finally got it straight that *these feelings had never had the power to hurt her and that she had never been "bad" to have sex feelings* that she began having the sexual satisfaction she needed to cement her relationship with her husband and make her marriage strong and sound.

One of the imperative jobs confronting the adolescent in order for him to mature wholesomely is to feel acceptable to members of the opposite sex. And yet, as we know, a person cannot feel acceptable to others unless he feels acceptable to himself.

Maturing is a complicated process. It involves many difficult, hesitant and apprehensive moments. Warnings that use fear to keep sex urges in check reinforce the fears which always accompany growing up and which are hard enough to endure. Condemnation of the sex urges to hold them under robs the individual of self-confidence. It adds obstacles to the task of integrating body and soul as the adolescent develops. Anything that makes him fear or berate or dislike his maturing body undermines the sense of his own worth which he needs so greatly to possess.

Sex education which leaves the adolescent with too heavy a fear of hurt or with the dregs of self-loathing destroys security in facing the world as a man or a woman. It lessens confidence in his capacity to find a vigorously satisfying life.

Implicit in the teen-ager's questions and wonderings lie complaints that the sex education he's had has attempted to stop him from believing that pleasure is permissible. It has failed to give him release from the fear that punishment must come as a result of enjoyment; that hurt or injury will result. It has failed to relieve him from self-condemnation. It has failed to answer his desperate need to like himself should he enjoy his body feelings and to know deeply and well that he is still a good person—with human dignity—and that enjoyment does not turn him from man into beast.

HOW TO CONTROL WHAT IS GOOD
NOT HOW TO DOWN WHAT IS "BAD"

It may seem paradoxical but it is also true that the teen-ager actually does not want so-called freedom until he is well advanced in his teens. He is uncomfortable with it. He wants to know with certainty that he can rely on the adults to help him erect and maintain proper controls.

The very strength of his impulses often makes him fearful that if left to his own devices he will be unable to manage them properly.

"Please can you tell me, are there shots the doctor can give you to keep you from getting too excited?"

"Are there certain thoughts you can think to hold you back?"

"If you eat more salt in your diet, or don't eat heating food like cooked cereals, will it help?"

But the handling of "good" feelings is very different from the handling of "bad" ones. For one thing, when a youngster feels that we condemn him, his back goes up in protest. This may make him want to get even by going against us and our ideals. He may run wild then, not so much because of the push of sex, but primarily because of the push of hostility and revolt.

Nor are controls and denials the same. Controls provide outlets. Denials do not.

"I got to do something about the sexy feelings. Isn't there anything that's all right?"

"Boys have wet dreams, but what are girls supposed to do?"

Here again we come up against a major complaint. The teen-ager's feelings are natural, yes. But in our society the mating wish is not sanctioned until the boy and girl are old enough to manage economically as well as biologically. What shall they do about the impulses meanwhile? Are there no right-feeling, sanctioned ways of managing them? Are there no legitimate action pathways along which sex urges may seek outlet during the time that it takes to grow up?

"When you're young," says Ned, philosophizing, "they teach you everything except what's most important. I think they ought to have you learn more about what you can do when you feel sexy instead of simply saying, 'Look! Turn it off!' To me that would have a lot more sense than diagraming sentences into grammatical parts."

The teen-ager is seeking new directions, getting oriented to a changing body; looking at creatures of the opposite sex with their changing bodies; visioning ahead to being husband or wife, father or mother, wondering about loving and being loved, not in the way of a child but in more growing-up and grownup fashion; feeling strange, frightened and eager all at once.

As we go on listening at length to our teen-ager's questions we become increasingly aware of what he wants and needs in his sex education. We see many profound and compelling wishes coming through the spoken words.

It's as if he were saying:

> *Give me facts with clear details,* **please.**
>
> > But don't stop here!
>
> *Discuss feelings also.*
>
> > Help me know that my feelings are "good," not "bad."
> >
> > Help me see that I am not "bad" for having them.
> >
> > Let me learn that I have the right to enjoy them.
> >
> > Help me get clear of the fear that they will hurt me.
> >
> > Free me from self-loathing and disgust.

And last but not least:

> Help me to know I can control the way I handle these "good" feelings instead of giving me blanket forbiddings and telling me my feelings are "bad" . . .

What we, as parents, do about these things is another story. It will depend on our personal philosophy, on what has gone before in the way of sex education and on how we can learn to build on what already has happened, not only in our teenagers' lives but in our own.

Meanwhile, one point, above others, stands brightly illumined:

> For SOUND SEX EDUCATION
> FEELINGS MUST BE CONSIDERED—
> not alone facts.

8. Sex Education Is More than Sex Information

When the teen-ager asks questions about sex and complains about lacks and omissions in his sex education, he is not only talking about what is happening in the present, he is also, either with or without knowing it, referring back to many things in the past.

If we are to handle well what we do with him now, we need to consider the past as well as the present. Our teen-ager is not just starting out in life. He has already lived a part of it. What we do now rests on what has already happened to him. The better we gauge its strength and weaknesses, the better can we carry his sex education forward. It's like building onto a house that has been partially constructed. We make a solid structure best, the more concretely we take into account the part that already stands.

Probably no one has ever attempted a house who hasn't said, "If I'd known in the beginning as much as I know now, I'd have planned this another way, or done that differently." Just so with our teen-ager's sex education: there are bound to be things we would have done differently. Weaknesses and mistakes are bound to have crept in. We make up for these best and strengthen most securely what remains to be built, the more clearly we take stock of what has gone before.

SEX EDUCATION BEGINS AT BIRTH

The sex education that a child obtains is much more far-reaching than we, his parents, ordinarily recognize. It includes not only what we have told him about the "facts of life." It includes many of the things he himself has experienced.

Adult sex, as we know, has to do with body feelings and also with love—with the spirit—with what goes on in a person's mind and emotions. Both body feelings and the mind's workings reach back to a human being's earliest days.

In the very beginning, the baby's body was all-important, as we've heard. He reacted then to the world and to the people around him in terms of his bodily needs and desires. He reacted primarily in terms of what made his little body comfortable or uncomfortable. Through his body he got first impressions about himself. These were already a part of his sex education.

The way a baby's mother touches him when he is newly born, this is part of his sex education. If she is tender and caressing, he begins his days with a sense that he is worth being loved. If she cuddles him with leisurely indulgence, taking pleasure in his pleasure, it lets him feel that enjoyment is a relaxed, happy thing.

On the other hand, if she carries on with diligent dispatch (as she has so often been told to do) with the focus on routines rather than on baby, she gives him quite a different feeling.

If a mother happens to be harassed (as many mothers have been in the stress and storm of a pressure-filled world) she can readily carry worries from other areas of life into life-with-baby, just as a father can carry worries from business into life-at-home. Then a child feels the intimacy of his first body close-

[97]

ness not as secure as it might be. He feels it fraught with tension rather than with the full acceptance he craves.

"But what can I do now?" moans Bob's mother. "Now that Bob's in his teens? I see the mistakes I made. I didn't even want him. His father had just been called into the service and I resented getting pregnant right then. I wasn't ready to have him and my resentment carried over after he was born. I know I didn't give him the acceptance or the cuddling he needed. And then, too, he hardly saw his father at all. I haven't wanted to say it or see it. What's the use now?"

However, the more clearly she saw it, the more fully could she cope with it. Denying it had kept her from seeing some of the things she could do belatedly to make up to Bob for what he had missed. Gradually she learned that the granting of closeness through understanding acceptance of feelings in adolescence can help make up for earlier lacks.

She set up periods for acceptant contact. "A couple of times a week, at least, I see that he has a chance to talk with me alone. Not with all the rest of the family around. When I took account of the time I spent with him before, I was appalled. Actually I had given him no real time! Sure, I said offhand hello's and how-are-you's. I asked questions about school and suggested a clean shirt or a hair comb. And I prided myself on the way we all carried on conversations together during dinner. But that was family time, not Bob's time. He was actually having none of the he-me-alone contacts which I'm sure now he had always missed. The sort of 'time alone' of one child and one parent that I read about somewhere. After all, you can't feel close or give out confidences with the other children te-heeing over the most sensitive bits.

"So now I say to them, 'Scoot! This is Bob's time, if he wants it.' His father does the same. Sometimes Bob turns us down. Sometimes he takes us up. Enough anyway, I guess, to make up for some of those earlier times he missed.

"As a result, he seems to be building self-confidence by leaps and bounds. And curiously he seems easier now, too, with his dates."

As for actual cuddling experiences to be had belatedly? Sometimes a dog or a kitten to cuddle will help bring the long-wanted sense of physical closeness. "That is," says Warren with nineteen-year-old dignity, "if you're still too young to cuddle a girl."

In any event, it's never too late to realize that early body experiences and contacts have had a part to play in the person's attitudes toward himself and toward sex.

But sex education is not a matter of body or *body feelings* alone. It is much broader. It involves relationships of person to person. Of liking, not liking, of loving, of hating. Of enjoyment in what one has of love fully given. Of missing what one has not. All the child's attachments as he grows. And the attachments to each other of the persons close to him. All of these have a role to play in what he feels and thinks and believes about sex.

The small child, for instance, senses not only the way his mother feels toward him but the way his father feels, too. Glad of having a family, or worn down with the burden.

He feels also the way his mother and father feel toward each other: This is the way a man and a woman are with each other —loving and warm, able to fight and to make up eagerly. Or superficially pleasant with the anger cold underneath.

He senses what goes on, whether they hide it or not.

Take Bernice, as example. When she was little, she felt her father's and mother's constant conflict, her father's evasion of responsibility, his attempts to escape elsewhere for solace of love without burdens. Although her mother never let Bernice see her crying, Bernice sensed the tears. Her mind picked up the actual facts and then went further. Her imagination elaborated on them and extended them to include the entire male sex . . . "All men are beasts." . . . "All men want to hurt women." These assumptions grew in her head, distorted from what was true about one man to untruths when applied to all men.

At nineteen Bernice bounded from one engagement to the next. Six times in the past year and a half she believed she had found her man.

"But always something gets in the way," Bernice told the psychologist. "I have misgivings. I pick out little flaws that are really unimportant. I exaggerate them dreadfully. I see this very clearly and yet I can't stop."

Finally, however, when Bernice understood that she had imagined falsely that all men were like her father, she began to see her men friends more realistically. She could separate fact and fiction in her mind and settle down to a comfortable marriage.

Bernice's story illustrates an important and neglected aspect of sex education which parents have known far too little about.

A child not only takes what he feels with his body and about his body as he grows; he not only takes what he feels about the relationships of person to person in his intimate world; but, in addition, he imbues these with his imaginings. Fact and fiction merge until, without knowing it, he is pushed by fiction as much as by fact.

Remember—

> Even more important than what has actually happened to him is what he has made of it in his own mind.

A small child takes even little things which, to the adult, logical way of thinking are silly, improbable or impossible. He transforms or expands these beyond all reason. He twines them about with wishes and threats that make him both ashamed and afraid. Many of the guilts and fears and failures of the adolescent are then due to holdovers from the childish thoughts and feelings he had in his earlier days.

One great weakness in providing adequate sex education for the teen-ager stems from our ignorance of the *barriers that lie in his own mind.*

If we are to do a good job
with our teen-ager's sex education
we need to
UNDERSTAND MORE ABOUT THE FANTASIES
he has had in the past.

FEARS AND FALLACIES

When the teen-ager asks us to help him clarify his sex feelings and to reassure him that they are all right, that he won't be hurt or punished, that they are not cause for self-loathing and disgust and that there are ways of control which need not bring the bereavement of complete denial, he is asking us to do what is impossible unless we have at least some grasp of his childish fantasies.

When we tell him about menstruation, about seminal emissions, about intercourse and having babies, the facts we give him may fall on a field so overgrown with the weeds of imagination that it is hard for the seeds of truth to take root.

When we try to set him straight on masturbation, we often run not only into what he has heard but also into what he has imagined.

When he propels himself into wild affairs, promiscuity or homosexual contacts, he is often still driven by his old unrealistic beliefs. In childhood these were natural. But he has failed to outgrow them. Impotence and frigidity, frightenedness or its cover-up of daredeviltry—these and many other problems can result and pursue him as he goes on.

[101]

Fortunately we have information today about the fantasies that are natural to persons as they grow up in our culture. This information comes from those who work most intimately with children and adolescents, as well as with adults who have been able to recover earlier feelings and thoughts. It contributes valuable knowledge to us who are eager to understand more deeply the youth whom we guide.

As we gain a sense of familiarity with the common fantasies that are part and parcel of children's normal development, we shall be better equipped to help our teen-agers move forward more successfully, accepting themselves and their own sex feelings with greater equanimity, assurance and faith.

HOW PRIMITIVE CAN ONE BE?

We have spoken of how children even in infancy sense their parents' feelings, especially their mother's. But we have not spoken of how strange fantasies begin to intrude. Although these have no shape in the beginning, nevertheless as the child grows his feelings rise from the vaporous past and take form in mind pictures as potent and hovering as the genie who emerged from the smoke of Aladdin's lamp.

When a baby nurses or is fed with his mother holding him warmly close, he gains through his mouth nourishing emotional contact as well as physically nourishing food. If either physical or emotional food, however, is insufficient to meet *his own particular appetite,* he frequently uses his mouth in biting attempts to get more.

Small two-year-old Nicky is panicked at sight of his mother nursing his new baby sister. "Mommie, Mommie," he cries, "don't let her do it."

"Don't let her do what, honey?"

"Don't let her eat you, Mommie. Don't let her eat you up."

Curiously, his mother reports that when Nicky, himself, was a baby, whenever she was hurried in nursing him, he seemed to feel it. "He'd grab till it hurt. Then I'd pull away and he'd grab all the harder. He'd bite and pull so hard, I felt *he* was literally trying to eat me." And now, here was Nicky accusing the baby of doing what his own little body had once seemed to do.

Whether the fantasy of eating Mother sprang up at sight of his sister or whether it was an echo from his own past, we do not know. But what we do know is that many boys and girls reach adolescence still full of love hunger. Even though their mothers may have given them what they considered to be a lot of loving, still they may not have received enough according to their own individually felt needs.

"I keep wanting and wanting," says Jim who is moving into his twenties. "I want more than any girl ever gives me. They call me 'greedy' and I guess I am. Sometimes I feel . . . well, how shall I express it? . . . like a baby, sort of, so starved he's voracious, and at other times, well . . . like a wolf. I frighten myself. Will I end up like Little Red Ridinghood's great-toothed grandmother? All set to devour the girl I'm after? I'd certainly be in a fine predicament. I wouldn't have her any-more."

What Jim says echoes what many small children feel and ex-press. They want Mother so badly they are hungry for her. They'd like to possess her completely—absorb all her atten-tion and time—absorb her entirely—devour her, as it were. But the pressure of their demands scares them. They are so voracious that they fantasy, as did Jim, that they may destroy the very thing they most want.

Normally in adolescence and in the prepubertal period, a child's physical appetite increases. He generally needs addi-tional food to take care of the additional growing. Many chil-dren are also more hungry because old fantasies are reawak-ened. "He's eating us out of house and home," Fred's mother sighed. "No matter how much he eats, he wants more and more." Through the food he takes in he is trying to satisfy emotional appetites and imagined cravings carried over from when he was a fast-growing infant.

During the adolescent spurt in growth, mouth cravings are apt to become important again. In addition to eating, it is common for the teen-ager to reemphasize other mouth habits. He chews gum incessantly. He smokes.

Sometimes as we meet these cravings with tolerance instead of condemnation, we lessen their importance.

This does not mean, however, that we have to pretend to like or approve, for instance, of a youngster's smoking if it goes against us. Our own convictions cannot be denied. If we believe it is harmful we shall have to say "No" and stick by it. On the other hand, we may have personal objections but we may go along with the opinion that in moderation smoking is probably harmless. This was how Sam's father felt. And so he said thoughtfully but without scolding, "I don't smoke, as you know, Sam, and I don't like it. But you and I are two different people. But a little of it, I'm convinced, won't hurt you. And I've a hunch if I forbid it, you'll do it anyway. Only be careful where and when you do it so it doesn't get you in wrong where you want to be in right . . ."

Sanctioning an act when it is not harmful helps decrease a youngster's need to do it as an act of revolt. This we know. Needless forbiddings are useless. They increase his sense of separation from us. They make him feel more deserted and lonely, more hungry than ever and more in need of finding some means with which to fill his lacks. Usually he disregards our forbiddings and gets around them somehow.

If we can talk with ourselves and come to the point where we feel real sympathy for his feelings, this may prove more useful.

The child who is hungry is hungry for what? Essentially for

more love. Therefore, as we met his struggle with a new kind of sensitive appreciation and understanding, we feed him what he is seeking. We give him some of the sustenance he craves. Perhaps enough so that he can let down a little and not struggle so hard in unfortunate ways.

However, voracious mouth cravings usually hold in them hostile and destructive fantasies. It's as if the person were saying, "I'm angry at you for not having fed me sufficient!" (Remember, even though you did, he may *feel* you didn't!) In consequence his anger may stand in the way of his accepting whatever you offer, or he may grab greedily at anything and everything and yet feel forever that he hasn't enough.

Sometimes, as you reminisce on the old hurts you gave him because of your mistaken ideas when he was younger, you may help him come out with feelings that are more wholesomely direct.*

Think back! Do you remember any mistakes you made and wish you hadn't—especially in connection with feeding or cuddling?

"I was terrible," says Cora's mother, "the way I used to let you lie in your crib and cry and wait for your bottle till the clock said it was the right time to feed you."

Fat Cora looked wise. "A baby would hate that. I must have hated it too. I know I hated it when you took desserts away from me later . . ." and she was off.

Many times when a child is obese, it is also wise to get help from a doctor who takes emotional as well as physical elements into account.

As the child goes through babyhood and early childhood, he moves his major focus to parts of his body other than his mouth.

* See Chapter 6.

Since we put enormous emphasis on bowel training in our culture, his evacuations become mysteriously interesting. Around their production he weaves many fantasies.

He discovers, for one thing, as did small Dick, that his mother is concerned if he soils or messes himself. With this discovery to the fore, Dick invariably messed himself at the

Sister: "What a mess you are!"
Brother: "Just take a look at yourself!"

very moment when his mother would start to feed the baby. It was as if he were saying, "I can get my mother away from all contenders by being a dirty little boy." In this he had an effective weapon with new ammunition always in storage.

As he grew, Dick became ashamed of his babyish maneuvers. In order to hide them even from himself, he went to the opposite extreme and became constipated. But in adolescence he still got his mother to focus on him by being, as she put it, "the filthiest boy you ever saw. He disgusts me," she said. "I get so fussed! He throws me into absolute fits."

Almost all adolescents are dirty. Sometimes this is a way, carried over from babyhood, of revolting or asserting independence. Within bounds it is part of the child's normal escape from being an echo of his parents into becoming HIM-SELF.

But if, through the excitement of fighting, it gains for him an exaggerated sense of power, it takes on fresh values which keep it going longer than it otherwise would.

Secretly Dick enjoyed his mother's fits. Because of her response, his messiness gave him power. At one and the same moment he could imagine himself triumphantly capturing his mother's attention and hurting her in retaliation for many imagined wrongs.

Dick's mother would have done better if she could have accepted his adolescent dirtiness for just what it was—a re-play of a baby's way of revolting from training pressures, as well as a living out of his earlier relish in messing.

She might have said with casual acceptance, but only if she could actually feel it, "You're as bad as a dirty infant," and let it go at that. Or she might have admitted her anger: "I'm mad at this mess, Dick!" And then have gone on to limiting the action outlets, still however, accepting Dick's baby feelings. "I know you like to be messy. In your own room, okay. But not in the living room. That's forbidden. *I* need to have that part of the house kept clean."

In addition she could have seen to it that Dick had recourse to more legitimate action pathways. Oil or poster paints, for instance, to mess with. Or a place in the attic or garage in which to collect junk or tinker messily with hobbies of his own.

The lure of many a hot rod is not only its roar, but the axle grease and the griminess under the car.

As it was, Dick's mother met his messiness with excited opposition to his actions and without constructive attention to his feelings. This only made Dick more excitedly opposed to her.

As he grew older he carried the same pattern into his relationship with girls. At eighteen he would throw them into fits with his dirty stories. At one and the same moment he would capture a girl's attention and fuss her; sometimes also disgust her. As with his mother earlier, he could fantasy himself a vanquishing hero with new ammunition always at hand.

But this failed to bring him deep satisfaction. It stood in the way of his achieving mutually given affection and love.

In the adolescent's attitude toward money, we may also find traces of a boy's or girl's earlier fantasies. When he pleads for more and more, never satisfied, the earlier love hunger may be coming out. In his unconscious imaginings he takes money as food to nourish him.

When he is stingy and hoarding, not only with money but with his possessions, he may belatedly be acting out his constipation. It's as if he were saying, "I have to hold on to this treasure in order to feel that I have in storage the ammunition I need to have to protect me and to enforce my demands."

Again it may help if we can provide opportunities for increased sharing and emotionally nourishing contacts as well as chances to let out the messiness through legitimate channels.

Sooner or later before a child is four or five, he discovers that the best feelings come from another part of his anatomy. His primary interest then moves, if all goes well, from the back to the front.

This is a tremendously important step. For unless the individual can know that this part of his body is good and clean and that enjoyment of it is good and clean, he may find it difficult ever to accept himself and his sex feelings as good and clean.

At this early stage in his development, a child also begins to notice his own anatomy and the anatomical differences between the sexes. He notices these even more if a baby of a different sex is born. Through observing things about the new baby, he also gets certain feelings about himself.

Have his parents wanted a girl or a boy? Their attitude toward the sex of the new sister or brother tells him about the acceptability of his own sex as well.

Linda's mother, for instance, touched Linda's baby brother gingerly. Inside herself she kept saying, "I'm not used to boys and their little gadgets. I hardly know how to handle Tim."

In nursery school, Linda, glancing over at one of the little boys at the toilet, turned to her girl friend standing beside her. "You and me and my mommie," she stated decisively, "we don't think boys are pretty at all."

Ordinarily, however, the awareness of male and female anatomy merges differently with our cultural slants. Unless the little boy is made ashamed of enjoying himself, he is proud of his body. He uses his prized male possession triumphantly. He can shoot straight into the toilet. He can make designs in the water, sprinkle the plants in the garden, try to squirt farther than other boys.

The little girl in our society does not feel superior, though she may act superior as a cover-up. Underneath she feels that boys are more desirable. Boys have something a little girl doesn't have.

"They've got those boy things," says Jean, who is ten.

The psychologist to whom she is talking nods in understanding.

Jean pauses a moment and then adds with a note of regret in her voice, "Girls don't have them."

"No, they don't."

"But," from Jean more hopefully, "girls do have babies and girls get things, too, somewhere else."

Her hands move to her still-flat little chest.

Jean is looking forward to getting something to substitute

[109]

for the "boy things." Perhaps they will give her the status she feels as a girl she has lacked.

If the little girl has touched herself, her hands have found confirmation of what her eyes have noticed and if she has furthermore gathered that touching is wicked, she may fear that the prized "boy thing" has been taken from her. She may figure then that she has been punished for the "wicked" sensations she has been "wrong" to enjoy.

"They took me to the hospital," says six-year-old Florence, "and they put me to sleep." She refers to the removal of her tonsils. "They took something out of my neck and my front. They did it because they didn't want me to touch any more. But," confiding anxiously, "I still got a little something left." When she touches this, however, she grows frightened. If she is discovered, it too may be taken out.

When the little boy touches himself and gets the impression that this is wicked, he becomes frightened also. Just as the girl may fantasy that something has happened to her, so the boy may imagine that the girl has had some dreadful mishap. If he follows his wicked inclinations, the same thing may happen to him.

"My big sister must have been very naughty," says small Rudy in grave consternation. "They cut her flat so she couldn't do it anymore. She bled . . ." He stops in fear.

Such fantasies are very common. They can hold far stronger sway in the child's mind than the facts we furnish about bodily differences. Buster looks very wise as he parrots, "Boys are born with it; girls are born without it." But when the school doctor comes around for vaccinations, he goes into tantrums. At the bottom of this lies a terrifying fantasy which he finally blurts out to the psychologist. "I don't want the doctor to make me into a girl."

Unwittingly we may have added our bit to this fear in either sex. "You'll hurt yourself, Del, if you touch yourself there!" Del forgets this. But she grows up unconsciously expecting to be hurt.

Sometimes the fear spreads to other parts of the body. The adolescent may then be cowardly. "I could shake him, he's such a sissy," one father explodes.

On the other hand, to cover his fear, a youth may turn daredevilish. "He flirts with death on his motorcycle!" to deny that he's scared.

Many little girls wish that they did possess the treasured "boy thing."

"I don't know what happened to mine." Four-year-old Marny looks puzzled. "But," more hopefully with an imaginary wish fantasy flashing into her mind, "I'm going to get another. I'm going to get one from my boy friend in nursery school. I'll wait till he's fast asleep and then he'll never know who picked it."

Some little girls make up fantasies of having hidden one of the desired objects away somewhere up inside.

"Only then when you get a baby," confided Patsy, "you burst open and lose it. I don't want ever to have any children at all."

Instead of wishing to have a family, Patsy prefers to be as much a boy as she can.

The idea of bursting or of being cut or hurt with the birth of a baby is not unusual. Neither are curious ideas about how the baby starts.

"Mother got a fat tummy," says Anna. "She musta eaten something to get a baby . . ." Anna is worried. She, too, would like to get a baby. But she is afraid.

For one thing, the pictures she has made up of impregnation and birth frighten her. In the way of many small children she imagines: Daddy fed Mother something and it grew inside her. Then her mind wanders further: What happens when you eat? Mother has explained that food comes out in bowel movements. The picture in Anna's mind is of a long tube that runs through the body from mouth to rectum with a sack in the middle where the baby grows . . . And finally, she figures, "the baby comes out when the mommie goes to the toilet. It comes out through the b.m. hole." . . . Only . . . and here terror creeps in . . . "The baby's so big. It can't ever get through. It will hurt the mother. Make her burst through her behind or out through her belly button . . ." Anna can't decide which.

Robby, whose mother is pregnant, is also frightened by fantasies similar to Anna's. Robby figures that when he grows up, if he gives a girl a baby, he will make her burst.

Madeline, at fifteen, is haunted by her earlier fantasies. She'd gone out with a boy and he'd kissed her. "He kissed me." The shades rise from the past. "Maybe I'm pregnant." She must stay away from boys and take no further chance.

LOVE AFFAIRS START LONG BEFORE SEVENTEEN

As boys and girls grow into adolescence, old wishes, fears and imaginings are bound to crop up inside them. Probably the most important of these date back to the first serious love affair which almost every child lives through during his first five or six years. It is the love affair that the little girl fantasies having with Father and that the little boy fantasies having with Mother.

It is a love affair that invariably ends in disappointment. A love affair that inevitably brings frustration. It must.

As it runs its course a child must learn to accept his littleness with its deprivations. At the same time, he needs also to gain a sense of still being worth while and beloved.

"My daddy likes me most," says small, blond Lisa, "because I'm a girl and he's portly to females." Already she holds the conviction that as a woman creature she is acceptable to a man.

"You mean partial," says her older brother amusedly.

"Daddy, yes, maybe. But not Mother. She likes boys the best."

These convictions as to the parents' partiality are not destructive but natural. The girl's wish to be Father's favorite is her first marriage dream. The boy's wish to be Mother's favorite is his.

When there are several boys or girls in the family, they will naturally vie with each other. In their own minds also each vies with the parent of his own sex.

Four-year-old Peter's designs are bold and bloody. "My daddy's leaving on the train tonight . . . The train is going to get wrecked. Then I'll be the daddy around here."

Walt, at nine, has not yet outgrown his rivalry. On his parents' anniversary after they have gone out to celebrate in the evening, he picks a red rose. Carefully he places it on his mother's pillow. Then he gets a ribbon and stretches it down the center of the double bed. At the foot, he prints a sign. "Congratulations! But, Daddy, stay on your own side."

Five-year-old Mabs, her mother reports, is a regular siren. "She flirts with her father from the moment he sets foot in the door. It's 'Rub my back, Daddy.' . . . 'Please, Daddy, smooth my hair.' . . . 'My arm's itchy, Daddy, scratch it gently.' . . . She crawls into bed with him practically every night."

But there came an evening when Mabs gave away the other side of the story. Her father was busy and seemingly ignored her. So she accosted him bitterly. "If you're too busy to pay attention to everybody, you better not pay attention to Mother. She's too old. You better only pay attention to me."

Obviously Mabs had in mind a fantasy of shoving Mother out and of taking her place.

But here grave danger enters. It is one thing to fight against brothers or sisters for supremacy. It is quite another to fight against a mother or father, especially when the child imagines wanting the big rival out of the picture.

[113]

The excitement Mabs had felt when she roughhoused with Daddy had been much like the excitement she had discovered in a certain part of her body when she had touched herself, in the same way as most children touch themselves. But Mabs had learned, as have most children, that touching is "bad." In her mind she put the two things together: The feelings you get when you touch are "bad." So the bouncy feelings with Daddy are "bad" . . . Especially since they were connected with the fantasy of getting rid of Mother . . . Mother would come and take Daddy away. She would take away whatever Daddy gave Mabs. And she might also hurt Mabs, injure her, do something nameless to the special place where the excitement registered. Do something fearful to her body . . . The very thought was too terrifying . . .

Mabs, like many other children, finally had herself thoroughly scared by her fantasies. To escape and deny them, she did a rightabout-face. Suddenly she would have nothing more to do with her dad.

"Your whiskers pinch me," she threw at him and shoved him away.

Meanwhile she clung afresh to Mother. She wanted now to climb into bed with her instead of with her father. "When I grow up, Mommie, you and I—we'll get married."

"Why, Mabs, you know girls don't marry ladies."

"But I want to, Mommie. And we won't have any old stickery men around."

Through making her father's whiskers a fence to keep them apart, she hid the fantasies of wanting him as husband. Through claiming excessive love for mother, she hid the mind-picture of shoving her out.

One more thing she did to bring comfort. She began eating constantly. And when she couldn't get things to chew at, she chewed at her nails.

[114]

In this Mabs was running back to the more babyish focus on mouth satisfactions to avoid the excitement-pleasure in that part of her body which had scared her too much.

As her father talked with the psychologist about the problem, he discovered many things.

"I see," he said, "I see among others that by tickling Mabs, bouncing with her and taking her into bed at night, I played up the very feelings she feared."

A baby needs physical closeness in the earlier periods of his life, with both father and mother cuddling him plenty. But in this period of love rivalry the body excitement of tickling and poking, of tossing and bouncing and of too much caressing is blown up by the child's wishful imaginings. He becomes stimulated beyond his capacity and becomes mortally afraid of his big rival's vengeance. He is filled with a kind of animal fear beyond all reason that he will be punished and hurt in that part of his body where the excitement has been most intense.

If he has had warnings against masturbation or threats because of it, he is apt to attach such warnings to these similar sensations.

Long before a child reaches adolescence there will then lie inside him several strands linking sex with hurt in his mind: If you touch, you will hurt yourself or hurt will descend on you . . . If you try to rival Mother or Father and shove out the one you are rivaling, hurt will come . . . If you're a girl and have a baby, you'll be hurt; or if you're a boy, you'll cause the hurt and you know well that if you cause hurt, you will bring hurt down on yourself too as punishment.

All children have feelings similar to Mabs'. They have the same urges and the same fears but ordinarily to a lesser degree. The overstimulation Mabs had received simply made her feelings more intense.

[115]

With some children still another source of fear may enter. Perhaps they have seen or overheard their parents having sex relations and imagine that Father is hurting Mother.

Or perhaps a child sees animals in the sex act. Says Nina, seven, excited but bothered, "He put his puppy seed into her backside." Like many another child she imagined that the rectum was being used and her mind jumped from animals to men and women and she concluded that with them the same thing occurred. Then disgust added itself to the fear.

If a child can live through the love-rivalry period, admitting the rivalry feelings and having them accepted and understood, he is fortunate. But once more actions and feelings need to be separated. He must have it made clear as crystal that actions which take Father from Mother or Mother from Father are of no avail. But this does not mean that his feelings are "bad." Quite the reverse. They are good and important. They plant a healthy desire to love and be loved later on by someone of the opposite sex.

Says Tad's father gently, "We know, Tad, there are times when you can't stand me, when you'd like me to disappear so you could be the boss around here. That's natural. All boys are that way. They'd sort of like to be their mom's husband and get rid of their dad. But Mom and I couldn't get along very well without each other. When you grow up, you'll be getting a girl of your own . . ."

Stell Smith's mother and father said nothing in particular. But their tolerance and warm interest in Stell's feelings said a lot for them. They were firmly entrenched in each other's affections and this was part of Stell's sex education. Stell's mother accepted her little girl's adoration of her father, and her father took it quietly, responding with kindly warmth but not seeking more numerous or greater displays of affection.

Stell's mother expected her child to be hostile to her out of jealousy for the place she held and which Stell coveted. Stell's father knew his little girl would also have her moments of hostility to him because he could not grant her what she imagined she wished. Both parents took Stell's displays of animosity with easy forbearance. They felt assured that if they permitted her these feelings, she would pass through the love-rivalry stage with greater security. She would shortly arrive at the day when she could admire and imitate her mother as a mother and not as a rival, and admire and love her father as a father and not as a longed-for sweetheart who turned her down.

Both smiled out of their own depth of love and understanding when Stell announced one day, "I'm glad I'm a Smith. There are so many Smiths in the world that when I grow up— what do you think? I can get myself a husband with Daddy's name."

During the love-rivalry period and out from the dim, dark infant past, these and other fantasies are universal. During adolescence, when man-woman relations again move to the forefront of the individual's mind and emotions, old desires and fears are apt to be rejuvenated. These may transfer from mother and father to sweetheart and lover.

If they prove too frightening instead of strengthening, the adolescent may hang back, unconsciously loath to take his place as a mature man or woman. He may remain essentially hesitant about sex feelings. He may, as protection, belittle sex because of old fears and shames. Perhaps then he runs back to the mouth pleasure of food and drink as the aim of existence, finding in them somehow a more dependent and dependable safety than in moving forward. Perhaps instead of love he seeks bigger and better productions, turning back the clock to the time when another kind of production gave him claim to fame. Perhaps he shuns contacts with the opposite sex as well as with his family, unconsciously afraid of loving any one person too much, afraid that another person may retaliate with injury and hurt. Or perhaps he goes berserk in sexual exploits trying to show by bravado that no fear exists.

In any case, it may prove comforting to us to know that what we have done is not altogether the cause of whatever problems confront our boys and girls. The thoughts and the fantasies which they invented earlier also play their part.

We can perhaps be more tolerant as we take this into consideration. We can then fulfill our role better in answering what they are after and in steering them safely into man's and woman's estate.

9. Putting In What's Been Left Out of Sex Education

We have seen by now that what we do in our teen-ager's sex education must consider his past as well as his present. And so please

NOTICE

Do not skip to this chapter if you have not read the last two. Do not turn to these pages if you have not read the first part of this book. You won't be able to make use of this as well until you've read the others. They are *musts* to give you the background for this chapter to mean what it should.

ABOUT MENSTRUATION

One mother explained to her daughter Nora, whom she noticed maturing, that when she got old enough to manufacture full-grown eggs which could grow into babies she would be a woman. "You'll be able to tell when it happens . . ."

"How?"

"Some blood comes out."

"You mean that's the signal?"

"Yes. It's a kind of signal that tells a girl she's growing up."

Came the day when Nora started to menstruate. She ran into the room where her parents were reading and triumphantly announced, "What do you know, Mother and Daddy? I'm making eggs."

Actually there are egg cells inside the body when a baby girl is born. Actually these cells only become mature enough to be fertilized somewhat after the onset of menstruation. Menstruation is a sign that a girl is well on her way to this ultimate goal of womanhood. But what was more important here than these technical details was that this child was taking this physiological transition from girl to woman in good emotional stride. Many do not.

Some girls in their unconscious minds imagine they are in some mysterious fashion being punished for earlier "badness" —for curiosities that should not have been there, for little-girl wishes to shove Mother out and possess Father or for touching themselves . . .

Threats they have heard in the past may now be catching up with them along with what they imagined when they first heard these threats.

Moans Paula, "Everytime I start flowing the thought jumps up in my mind, 'See, I've been hurt.' "

"That may be my fault," says Paula's mother. "I used to warn you not to touch yourself for fear you'd make yourself sore. I was full of those awful scare stories my mother told me. But I've learned lately that they don't hold an ounce of truth."

Some girls do not feel ready to grow up. They may unconsciously wish still to be babies. Or they may hope that by staying babyish they will manage still to get some of the things they have wanted and missed.

Cramps and nausea, aches and sick feelings may be signs of hidden unhappiness about turning from child into woman. Neither the coddling nor the belittling treatment does any good. Listening to the girl and giving her opportunities to talk about herself, on the other hand, may.

Idabelle complained every month. Her mother, before she knew better, would bring on hot drinks and hot bottles. She would dismiss her daughter's moans and groans with supposedly encouraging phrases. "You'll be all right in a few hours. And anyway, dear, this is nothing! Just wait till you have a baby. That really is grim."

Finally, however, Idabelle's mother learned better. She learned about helping a child get out troubled feelings.

"If your child feels mean, give him a chance to get the mean feelings out. That can reduce them. Talking's a good way for the adolescent youngster . . .

"If your child is afraid, *give him a chance to get the fear feelings out* . . . Don't probe. But don't turn him off either. Let him complain and see what comes.

"Be interested in his troubles and worries. Maybe along with the griping some of the more bothersome thoughts will slip out. If not, your willingness to listen may of itself do more than you think."

So Idabelle's mother figured, "I'll give it a try."

"Oh," groaned Idabelle with a sour look on her face. "I feel so awful!"

"I know how it is," said her mother, drawing up a chair and settling back to listen, real interest showing.

"I hurt so in my middle!" Idabelle moaned. "I wish I'd feel better. I just can't miss school . . . I can't miss the tennis tournament . . ." She paused a few moments and then, very angry, she exclaimed, "Why on earth did you make me be born a woman? I'd have avoided all this misery if you'd only let me be a boy!"

Idabelle raved on until, as suddenly as the complaining had started, it stopped. Idabelle burst out laughing. "Gee, Mom, did you ever hear anything half so absurd?"

"Yes, I have," Mother answered. "Me! I've painted a woman's life in pretty grim colors, as if men had all the advantages . . ."

"Well, they have, haven't they? Look at Jack. He never gets this 'curse.' He goes more places with Dad. He plays tennis twice as easily. Beside which I think you've always preferred him . . ."

"It's true that mothers do have a special kind of feeling toward their sons. But they also love their daughters in a different way."

That was all for the moment. However, with additional opportunities for voicing the fantasies that she would have been more beloved and happier if she'd been a boy—Idabelle grew less incensed about her "horrible fate," and her pain eased.

Even though no "revelation" ever rolls out, acceptant listening that communicates understanding can sometimes of itself bring more relief than do pills.

Many parents believe it wise to check with the doctor if a girl continues to have trouble with her periods. Seldom does the doctor find anything physically wrong. But he can sometimes step in and give the girl opportunities to talk in a more casual and easy way than the parent, who is naturally more emotionally involved. Only under very rare circumstances and only if the doctor finds unusual and severe symptoms should there be actual examination of the sex organs. For the young girl starting out on her course of being a woman such an examination more frequently than not stands as a very grave and shocking threat, as a punishment for secret thoughts, as an invasion of privacy and as a violation of her whole person.

Irregularity in menstruation is very common. Sometimes girls skip several months in between each of their first few periods. Most women remain somewhat irregular and can expect at least a third of their cycles to extend past the time they believe it is due. The idea that one has to be regular to be normal sets up tension which, in its turn, like other worries, may cause delay.

"I'm late," wails young Jinny. "And I know my mother'll think the worst. She never trusts Bob and me. She watches me like a hawk, expecting me to skip . . ."

The worry made young Jinny late just as an intense desire to be pregnant has made many a woman late, or the intense desire not to be pregnant. Letting down on tension often does wonders. Talking out worries to an acceptant listener may help to bring this about.

Prior to the onset of their menses, many girls are worried about personal hygiene and want information concerning it. Showing them, if they wish, just how to wear their napkins instead of merely telling them can make for a bit of needed assurance. However, insisting on such demonstration if they wish to avoid it becomes an invasion of the privacy they crave.

Discussing the matter of bathing and of exercising is also in order. "Many girls go swimming, bathe, take showers, play tennis and enter into other games as usual. Many girls prefer not to do strenuous things. Ordinarily, it depends on psychological choice rather than on physical necessity . . ."

Boys are fully as curious, and often as worried, about menstruation as are girls.

"But why on earth are they so callous?" one mother complained. "When my daughter has her period and doesn't feel like swimming, her brother starts in on her: 'What's the matter?' . . . 'What's happened to you?' . . . 'Why don't you get in the water? You're chicken! What's wrong?' . . . I've told him girls have what's called their period once a month and during that time he should be more considerate. But I might as well talk to a lizard for all the attention he pays."

Often a boy's callousness is his way of covering his worry. He has heard and seen things. This is mysterious business: Something wrong! Bleeding. And blood stands for hurt.

Then old, unreasoning mind pictures come crowding . . .

Most often, if he dares ask what he wants, he will ask, as many girls also want to question: Where does the blood come from?

He may be interested then to hear that there is a sack inside the girl where her babies will eventually grow and that this gets a new lining every month after the girl reaches a certain age. The new lining keeps it freshly prepared and ready for the baby to root in, just as a plant roots in fresh soil. In consequence the sack, or uterus, sheds its old lining every month and the shed lining is naturally bloody.

But very seldom will this be sufficient. He may feel like thirteen-year-old John, who exclaimed, "My goodness, a woman spends a lot of her life preparing for babies. It's an awful waste of energy, isn't it?" And like John, he may go on with endless questions or, like others, turn callously away to hide anxiety that has not been allayed or curiosity over which he still is ashamed.

When a youngster asks, "Where does the blood come from?" he often means "Where does it come *out of?*" To us this may seem to make very little difference. But to him it is all-important. Because in his mind, stowed away from times past, lies the imaginary child picture of wounds, of the little girl's body born like the boy's and then being mutilated as punishment for that "bad" business of touching or for other "bad" feelings and thoughts.

He fears now that the blood may be coming out of this old wound. What he is seeking is another mind picture to replace this, so that he may know that the ancient, childish belief is not true.

Some boys and girls have only a vague notion of physiology.

[124]

Some of the younger teen-agers are unbelievably naïve—unaware even that there is such a place as the vaginal opening. The boy figures that the girl has the same number of openings as he has. And the girl, having been warned against "touching," has either ignored the vagina or has forgotten its discovery at an earlier age.

And so parents are wise to include a description of the girl's external anatomy, even if this is a "repeat."

When Ron asked his mother where the blood came from, she answered, "The girl has a special opening. She's born with it. Every woman has it! It's not the bowel opening; and it's not the one the urine comes from either . . ."

"Hmph!" said Ron. But his relief was very evident.

Like others, Ron felt: Since a special sort of place had been provided, no other organ was in danger . . . Therefore his organs were safe.

Frank's father went even further. He noticed Frank's tense, nervous jigglings and the sidewise glances he cast at his sister when she stayed off the tennis court.

Later, he made opportunity for Frank to be alone with him. "I noticed you looking at Sis today," he said in opening the subject. "I thought perhaps you were wondering why she wasn't playing."

"Yes, Pop, I was. Mother told me something about a 'period' or whatever it's called. I didn't get it. Only, I have been wondering if it hurts her . . ."

"No, Frank. But I can understand your asking. Perhaps you've noticed that she bleeds and you very naturally connect blood with being hurt."

"Uh-huh. I saw some blood in the bathroom and it got me scared."

His father nodded. "Plenty of kids worry about girls and their anatomy. When I was a real little kid I used to think my sister had something missing. That it got cut off somehow. And

[125]

when she started to bleed I thought it was from the old wound. Something like that! It's silly, but a lot of children imagine that sort of stuff. Not an ounce of truth in it. But it's what they think."

"I never thought anything that silly!" Frank scoffed. Nevertheless both his father and mother noticed that he seemed easier about his sister's periods after this talk.

ABOUT BIRTH

Knowledge about the "third opening" is relieving also when it comes to the worries over birth.

"I couldn't see how the baby was going to get out of either of the other two holes," young teen-age Betty confides. "It makes a difference, though, knowing you've got such a stretchable place."

Her mother nods, "I used to think I'd burst when I had a child. Before I knew there was an opening that could stretch wide enough to let the baby through . . ."

"I used to think . . .

"I used to think . . ."

Betty chatters on, and Mother listens, adding just enough about her own former childish ideas to let Betty feel that she herself was not strange, different or "bad" because of what she had felt and thought.

"You can help lay the ghost of these earlier fantasies by talking about them," Betty's mother had learned.

"It must hurt all the same, Mom. Doesn't it—just terribly —when the baby gets born?"

"It used to, in our grandmother's day. It still did in mine. And I guess in some instances it does now. But doctors have developed new methods of pain killing. And there are ways, too, of exercising and preparing one's muscles during pregnancy that make it possible to have what's called 'painless' or 'natural childbirth.' There are books about it one can get."

"Before I have a baby, I will."

Then, after a moment, "Mother, . . . tell me . . . something else I've wondered about for the longest time. Doesn't it bother you to have a baby pulling at your breasts when it feeds?"

"I used to think it would, so I didn't nurse you children. But I wish now I had. They say it feels good."

"You mean to the mother?"

"Yes. Sort of thrill-y and cozy and warm."

Betty glanced toward her mother, her face illumined. This was something new and wonderful, having mother talk about good feelings that could come to one's body. She sighed contentedly, "Gee, Mother! And I'll bet it feels good to the baby too."

HEALING OLD HURTS

Betty's mother here has done something tremendously important. She has *put good body feelings in the category of being good*. She has lifted from them the old onus of being wicked and "bad." She has attached them to the warm and lovely yet primitive act of mothering in which body and spirit combine. And she had admitted to wishing that she might have got more of these feelings herself.

She smiled back at Betty. Then she went on. "I've learned that lots of things feel good to babies and children and to big people, too. Things we've been told we should be ashamed of. I've found out we shouldn't be at all!"

Betty stared at Mother, her eyes round and big. "What do you mean?" with a catch in her voice, eager yet somewhat afraid.

"I, too, felt my heart getting a little poundy," her mother confessed when she told of the experience. "But I decided I wasn't going to let Betty go on as I had—so stupidly ashamed of everything human. So I barged ahead! I tried to remember

[127]

all the mistakes I had made in needlessly stopping Betty from enjoying her body. At the time, of course, I thought I'd been right. But why let old mistakes stay uncorrected? Especially when something as vital to your child is at stake."

Betty's mother thought back. "When you were little," she said, "I was a thumb snatcher, for one thing. I've learned now that it doesn't hurt jaws or mouth for a small child to suck. But I did everything to you then to make you stop.

"And then I was a dessert holder-upper. Custards and apple sauce and the other nourishing, sweetish foods your little body enjoyed with its taste buds! 'No,' I'd say. You couldn't have them unless you ate all the things you didn't like first. That was foolish too.

"But worst of all," and here Betty's mother drew a deep breath, "when you began to touch your tee-tee, which is the thing that feels best of all, why I had fifty-nine cat fits. I've found out since that it's harmless and I could have saved both of us a lot of worry. But I didn't know then . . ."

"You mean"—Betty's mouth hung open—"it's not true that it drives people crazy? Nothing terrible happens to them?"

"No. Not one single terrible thing. It's perfectly natural and normal and I was a very foolish woman ever to have made you think anything else."

In this, Betty's mother was bringing out what has been well established: We know now that masturbation does not injure a person or make him "nervous." We know, however, that anxiety, fear and shame over it often does.

Many an adolescent has acquired just such feelings! They intrude into the respect he has for himself as a person. And this is often what hurts him most.

At the stage where the adolescent now finds himself, sex impulses, as we know, surge freshly. The sight of a girl or a boy to a member of the opposite sex, the sound of a voice, the thrill of a chance touch, daydreams of love and romance—all bring body sensations akin to the earlier ones that were "bad." Just as the love-rivalry "bad" feelings and the touching "bad" feelings got attached to each other earlier, so the adolescent love surgings get attached now. Like a snail pulling in its horns, the boy or girl may retreat from healthy contacts. Or he may run wild to prove to himself that anxiety has no foundation.

Betty, sighing: "Oh dear! It's hard to wait!"

What Betty's mother was doing was trying to reassure Betty that fear and anxiety and shame of body enjoyment had no place.

THEY WANT PLAIN TALK

Without thinking, Betty's mother had slipped back to the baby term "tee-tee" that Betty had used in bygone days. Talk of this part of the body had since then faded out of the picture. Betty had never acquired any other term. And so, when Betty's mother referred to it now, she did what came most naturally.

After listening to a speaker recently another girl in her late teens went up eagerly to the platform. "What a relief it was," she confided, "to hear you talk so simply about the things that others are so stilted about. It was good to have you use our language."

Had Betty been accustomed to the word "vulva," it would have been a different matter. As it was, the most comfortable expression for both Betty and her mother was the baby word. And so Mother's use of it in the beginning facilitated their talk. Later she was able to work in as synonyms the more scientific names.

Not infrequently language difficulties get in between parent and child and slow down communication.

Long before adolescence most children have talked with other children and have acquired their own vocabulary. By the time they are in their teens, these youngsters ordinarily have used colloquial terms among themselves. This is the language in which their imaginings and wonderings are set. As one boy put it, "We want to ask about things in the way we think about them to ourselves."

But if by chance some of these words slip out, parents are prone to grow indignant.

"P-lease, Bud, stop that gutter talk . . ."

"Heavens! Lucille! Where on earth did you hear such horrible words?"

The adolescent feels taken aback. Here is an extra stumbling block thrown in his path when he is trying so hard to find his way among conflicting ideas, supposed truths, superstitions, facts, and feelings.

He craves the familiarity of whatever language is most familiar. He likes also to feel that we are using language that is comfortable to us and that comes out of the homeyness of intimate usage, not out of a textbook lecture prepared just for this occasion and as distant as the moon and the stars.

For years in books about child psychology and sex education, parents have been told to use a scientific vocabulary. But with added observation and more vivid and direct contact with children's actions and fantasies, the eyes and ears of those who work most searchingly with them have become more perceiving.

All of us know that the mechanics of translating a foreign tongue can interfere with an understanding of what is said. Curiosity then goes unanswered. This is often what happens when we reply to our children's questions in words that are foreign and often strained. We answer technically but we leave their curiosity hanging in mid-air.

We adults very commonly use some of the same common terms as our children. And yet we avoid these terms assiduously when we talk with them.

Perhaps we should ask ourselves: Are we afraid of revealing dark secrets and shames? We needn't be. After all, gutter meanings do not lie in the words of themselves but only in whatever gutter thoughts we connect with them.

Our own use of these words has probably not been gutter usage. We have probably spoken them in moments of hearty and wholesome love talk and love play.

Without realizing it, however, by avoidance or indiscriminate condemnation, we may put needless barriers in the way of our children's free questioning and of our making things clear. We may once more give a youngster the impression that his terms are not nice and that he is not nice.

We can gain confidence better by saying, "There are lots of words for these." Then we can go on and name several of them and by so doing show that the lowly words he has most probably heard do bear mention as well as the more scientific synonyms. "I've called it by such and such term—what have you called it?" Or "These are my words for it—what are yours?" Or "Here are some of the words I've heard used. How about you?"

If we can show him that we are interested in what he has

been calling things and are willing to listen, he may bring out his wonderings more readily since he can express them in his own vernacular. This may be distinctly personal. Or it may be the group language used in his particular set or locale.

We may fear, however, that if he uses these words with us he will grow *too* free with them elsewhere and fling them about.

But judging where and when to use certain terms is not new business in his life. Nor is it new business in our dealings with him. 'Way back when he was little we shushed him in company when he spoke about toileting. More recently, when we started applying the newer ways of discipline, we talked with him about confining his criticisms of us and his gripes against us to the privacy of our company alone. "Lots of people misjudge you when you talk in public, for instance, about being angry. They think children should always be respectful, never mad at their parents. And they think mad-talk exceedingly bad. When we're alone it's all right; but not in company."

The same sort of thing applies now. Said Randy's father, "Lots of people misjudge you when you talk like this. Many grownups believe these words are dirty. As you know, many children do too. They do have dirty meanings. But some of them have love meanings also. It all depends on how you use them. . . . I'd be careful though, because you don't want to be branded foulmouthed by people, young or old, who consider them foul."

Randy looked thoughtful and answered, "You know, Dad, you said an awful lot then. It's strange but I can usually tell whether it's the dirty use or the clean use that a person intends."

"And sometimes you want to ride along with the dirty use as well as the clean one?"

"That's true. It seems sort of smart."

[132]

At least it fits in with the revolt need that many an adolescent feels intensely. When he uses these terms smuttily, this frequently serves as outlet for hostility. Forbidding won't accomplish much. But understanding may. The terms are then no longer expressly forbidden. His use of them is no longer a gesture of throwing his parents' veto to the winds.

IF EASY-DOES-IT COMES HARD TO US

Ideally what our boys and girls want is someone who can talk with them comfortably about sex. Someone who is not embarrassed. Someone who becomes neither bothered nor excited over the subject. Someone who is easy within himself.

We have repeatedly read these specifications! They are the ideal ones no doubt. But we haven't been brought up ideally. And not many of us can reach this ideal.

However, there are some things we can do to help us feel at least somewhat more comfortable.

The first of these takes us back to the matter of language. Betty's mother used the funny old little-girl term. That made her feel more comfortable because it was more familiar. On the other hand, for some people the less familiar words are the more comfortable ones. In speaking of bodies, for instance, some feel easier using such terms as "vulva" to designate the whole external female genital area, "vagina" for the opening and the channel inside, "clitoris" for the "small, humpy place that has such good feelings," as one girl described it, and "penis" and "testicles" or "testes" for the male organs.

And so as the first step to help get *you* at ease, *choose whatever terms are the most comfortable for you.* (In spite of the advantages to your child of using familiar terms, your maximum comfort—which may be shaky anyway—comes first!)

The next thing is to *be frank about your feelings concerning the terms your child uses.* If you can accept them sincerely, so much the better, as we have said. But *don't be insincere.* In-

[133]

sincerity makes you less comfortable. Moreover, your distaste will be sensed and will become a deterrent to frankness between you.

It's better to stop your child if his language distresses you (even though you know again this isn't ideal). One mother said, for instance, "I know you and some of your friends use those words. But I don't personally. And I've never liked them. I get too embarrassed. So let's not, around me."

Supply your teen-ager with words if he fumbles. But don't make your condemnation of his words an over-all, indiscriminate business. Let him know you know that some people use such terms decently and that your feelings against them are personal with you.

This brings us to another point: *If you feel embarrassed on any score in talking about sex, better say so!*

Right straight out: "I feel uncomfortable talking about sex! I wish I didn't. But I do."

"I still feel a bit tense!" confessed Betty's mother, when Betty came with more wonderings several months later. "When it comes to the sixty-four dollar question that we've never really gone into . . ."

Betty giggled. "Yes, Mom, you've always blushed whenever we've come within miles of that one! We almost got to it a couple of times and I could feel you backing away."

"Or turning and running!"

Then Betty's mother managed something else that held value. You can try this one also: *Be frank about the mistakes and embarrassments of the past instead of evading them.*

"Like the time you spelled out that four-letter word and asked me what it meant!"

"Yes," nodded Betty. "You got red as a beet and said I shouldn't say anything so horrible ever again. So I made up my mind I'd never ask you anything again! My! I was mad . . ."

"Uh-huh," thought Betty's mother. She knew, as you no

doubt also know by now, that it's good to: *Let your child get his old hostilities out for all the times you have not attended adequately to his sex education.* It may help clear the air and make him more friendly. And if he's more friendly you'll be more relaxed.

"After all, I felt hostile to my folks for holding out on me. Why shouldn't Betty feel angry at me for having held out on her?"

She hadn't forgotten, and you don't need to either, that it helps to: *Try recalling how you felt when you were young.* This can bring more understanding of how your child feels right now.

Out loud Betty's mother continued: "I was stupid to renege on that most important question!" Once more acknowledging her mistakes.

"Yes, you were," Betty agreed, the bitterness quite apparent.

"You didn't like me at all for it." Mirroring Betty's feelings.

"No, Mother, I didn't. If you'd told me things straight out, you could have saved me from a lot of worry and fretting . . ."

"I realize it, darling. But believe me, I didn't know enough to then."

"But you're doing all right now!" Betty's smile was radiant. "And it's twice as hard, I know, when you've had parents as old-fashioned as yours."

Then with rapport reestablished Betty confided, "I still have a lot to get straight. The basic facts—those I've managed to pick up. But there are so many details I can't figure out . . ."

As Betty went on, Mother found herself listening and answering with fewer qualms than ever before.

When it comes to you and your child, if, after thinking everything over, you still feel you don't want to, or can't, go

[135]

into such discussions, if you feel that you would be too uncomfortable in coping with such questions—*don't drive yourself.*

You can possibly find someone else for your child to talk
with. A doctor. A psychiatrist. A minister. (There is a whole
group of pastors these days interested in psychology.) A family
counselor. A psychologist. A gifted teacher.

Or, if you choose, you can go to someone for yourself. To
help you revamp your own attitudes. You can, for example,
join a group where parents can discuss their own feelings
under trained leadership in an endeavor to become easier and
more comfortable inside.

However, there may still be a hurdle, not in you but in your
child.

Even though you get past your own old prejudices, it still
may be hard for your child to discuss these matters with you.
His feelings may get in the way more than with a person about
whom he cares less. For one thing, he will perhaps feel less
concerned with a more distant person's opinions of him should
he reveal thoughts he has believed were "bad." For another
thing, he may find it easier to talk to an outsider since many
of his sexual worries and embarrassments arose originally from
imaginings that were born out of his relationship with you,
his parents, in bygone days.

ABOUT INTERCOURSE

In any case, if you and your teen-ager do manage to talk
frankly together, sooner or later you will come to the question
of sexual intercourse.

Like Betty, your child will doubtless have managed to
gather the general facts. So also has Craig.

"The man puts his penis inside the woman," he states concisely. "I know that. But just where?"

Like Craig and like Betty, your child also will be after de-

ı'll do well to explain in your
ble way. Don't be afraid to
.e. And when you don't know,
h a promise to consult book or

You know now that to either boy or
nowledge that a woman has a third open-
.ial channel or tube leading up from it to the
where her babies will grow. (We've talked about this
already.)

"How is it done?" . . . You know this too.

"How often?" . . . It depends . . .

"But" said Nell, "you can't have that many babies."

"It isn't done every time to have a baby," her mother assured her. "It makes two people who love each other dearly feel closer and more intimate, more at one with each other. It's done for love many times . . . How often depends on how they both feel."

"How *do* they feel?" . . . Here is the tough one, the one at which the boy or girl invariably seeks to arrive if he dares.

But after you've considered it, you'll see that this one isn't too difficult either!

You'll need first to recognize what the adolescent is really after.

Actually he knows how it feels. He has known a long time.

The answer that your teen-ager usually wants to this question is not information or fact, but sanction for the feelings he has had in touching himself. For he intuitively knows inside him that these feelings are like those he will have in intercourse. He is now after reassurance; to know that his feelings are normal, healthy and good.

When Betty came to this question, her mother answered, "Those feelings? You know them. They're like when you look at a romantic scene in the movies or like when you touch yourself. Only even better. Because you're together with someone you love."

In this simple way of putting it, Mother shows Betty once more that Betty's experience with similar feelings has been wholesome and sound.

Betty gazed thoughtfully out of the window. And then she said an astonishing thing.

"That helps a lot, Mother. I'd been wondering whether I could hold out till I got married. Lots of girls don't. I think they're curious. Now that I know what it feels like, I won't have to do so much research."

"My!" thought Betty's mother, "haven't both of us grown up tremendously since we've talked on and off about these things over the last couple of years?"

How to help these adolescents not to be driven to do so much research? How to help them feel secure and satisfied enough to maintain controls? This is probably the biggest of all questions in the minds of parents. It, too, is part of what must be included in the sex education of today's youth.

So let us turn to it next and consider it in the context of rising interest in each other that boys and girls feel at this age.

10. The Other Half of the Human Race

BOY MEETS GIRL

No doubt the problem of most concern to most parents during their children's adolescence has to do with boy-girl contacts. There are practical, down-to-earth parts to this. Parts that deal with behavior and conduct—with how a boy or girl ACTS.

There are other parts to it also. Parts that have to do with how a boy or girl FEELS.

Too often we talk about and work with the first part only. For feelings related to the sex drive have long been hard for us to deal with.

As a result, we are inclined to focus on how our children *behave* in their boy-girl relations. We are inclined to by-pass how they *feel*. It's as if we were expecting them to handle their feelings automatically by the attention we pay to their acts.

As with other things, however, we do better if we pay attention to both.

At the beginning of the puberal cycle, a small gland—the pituitary gland—located at the base of the brain sends out a secretion called the gonadotrophic hormone. This in its turn sets off growth of the sex glands, the testes in the boy and the ovaries in the girl. It stimulates them to produce sex hormones or endocrines of their own and eventually to manufacture mature sperm cells and egg cells.

The puberal cycle with these internal changes starts long before puberty proper. Though the girl's first menses ordinarily come between twelve and fourteen, the changes inside her body start anywhere from nine to twelve; sometimes even as early as eight. Though boys ordinarily have their first seminal emission around thirteen or fourteen, the internal changes begin between ten and a half and twelve, in some boys even as early as nine.

As the internal changes progress, the outward changes come. These we notice as we observe our teen-ager's growth. They proclaim to the world and to the opposite sex that childhood is being left behind. Here, for all eyes to see, finally stands a woman. There stands a man.

The puberal cycle, however, does not stop with puberty. Internal changes and often external growth continue for several years.

It is probably a combination of the physical changes, the sight of the opposite sex growing into maturity and the perception of one's own development that brings the upsurge of sex feelings and the increased interest in sexual concerns.

When boy meets girl in the early teens, hesitance is usual. On her part the girl is giggly and coy. She whispers and titters and has secrets with her girl friends. She seemingly shuts boys out. Perhaps this is because she is thrown together in school and elsewhere with boys her own age. These boys seem "babyish" and beneath her, since they are normally slower to develop. Till about fifteen, they are apt to be smaller. Their beards are pinfeathering and their voices quaver.

[140]

With disdain, the girl looks down on them. "That Bob! Those boys! They won't dance. They won't do anything!" with a snort. "They don't know a horse from a cow. They don't keep their ears clean. They actually smell!"

Teacher: "George, I've been calling on you."
George, waking up: "Oh, gee! I wasn't here."

But give the same girl a chance at some more mature and noble-looking creature, then her interest crops out. "That Roy! Have you seen him? Let's face it, he's terrific! He's six feet tall if he's an inch. He simply walked away with the class election. I tell you, he rates! Only, do you know? One of the girls said he wanted to kiss her the second time they dated. That's rushing it too much. But still, let's face it, he's cool!"

Nevertheless, if she suddenly finds her Adonis seeking her out, quite unexpectedly she may retreat.

Ruth has been dying and sighing to be asked to the dance in the gym by a boy two grades ahead of her. However, when the invitation actually materializes, Ruth turns it down. "I was crazy to go," she exclaims, "but I couldn't. I'm crushed. I've never had such a bitter disappointment. What happened? Why can't I go? Don't forget there's that tremendous assignment we got in English. Miss Zee's a mean one. If I don't get it done, well, you know . . ." lamely trailing off.

On his part, the boy in his early teens characteristically sneers or teases or turns on his heel at sight of girls.

George, who is thirteen, says with contempt, "The girls in my class think they're real cute. They act real conceited and real glamorous. But when you try to talk to them they just ignore you and act so big shot they give you a pain."

Mike can't see his older sister for dust. From his thirteen-year-old viewpoint he belittles her attractiveness and doesn't see why any of the boys want to take her out. But one evening he sticks his head into her room to call her to the telephone and catches her half dressed. In spite of himself, young Mike lets out a whistle. "Oh, boy! Bosoms!" he exultantly exclaims.

Actually both boys and girls are tremendously conscious of the other sex and are reacting with body feelings that frighten them.

The boy, seeing the girl of his own age as more of a woman than he is a man, often unconsciously identifies her with "Mother." The earlier love-rivalry feelings then come rushing. His jeers then serve as self-protection to make himself keep himself away.

Somewhat later when he falls, he usually falls for a girl much older. This still is protection. He knows that "older women" are quite out of sight.

Similarly the girl entering her teens who yearns for an "older man of about seventeen" still holds the picture of an idealized father in mind, so that she is ordinarily her own dictator in insisting for herself that the arm-length policy prevail. She will hang on to the telephone betraying her interest in everlasting conversation *about* boys at first, and later *with* them. But she still must keep the distance safely between.

This might be termed the period of avoidance. A pause, as it were, in which to build courage.

Some boys and girls seem to skip this period. Some go through it before they reach their teens. But when it exists with its various incompatibilities of boy wanting older girl and girl wanting older boy and the older ones of both sexes looking down on the younger ones, there are resultant barriers which either bother parents or let them breathe a sigh of relief.

Thirteen-year-old Dave's mother was one of the bothered ones. She was overconcerned with her son's lack of interest in girls. She arranged for him to go to dancing school. She invited girls over. She surprised Dave with a "gorgeous Valentine party," and kept urging Dave to "be nicer to girls."

However, when he crawled inside himself, becoming more morose and truculent, she decided she had better get inside herself for a change, at least for long enough to do some soul searching.

"Yes,"—she came up with a good discovery—"when I was twelve or thirteen, my older brother wouldn't pay the least attention to me. I was utterly crushed. I see I've been identifying myself with the girls Dave neglects; as if I were in their boots, once more being neglected myself. I've been thinking of them and not of how Dave feels at all."

The change that followed in her attitude helped Dave to be franker and more open.

"Girls," he confided to her, "they're just impossible."

"I know." She nodded, feeling with him at last. "I know they make for a lot of problems."

[143]

"They sure do for boys."

His mother's mirroring of his feelings was far more helpful than her earlier proddings. It left him freer, when he became ready, to move ahead at his own speed.

Father: "Wasn't it last week you were so anti-girls?"
Son: "But, Dad, I'm older now!"

In contrast, some parents try to delay things and are pleased if their youngsters are not concerned with the opposite sex. "He's got plenty of time to go with girls!" Or "I'm grateful, believe me, that she doesn't care about boys yet. I'll have enough trouble on that score later."

The age at which boys and girls become outwardly interested in each other does vary. So—be watchful and tolerant. And in early adolescence, don't try either to hold back your child or to push him on in his contacts.

Let your young teen-ager's
INTEREST IN THE OPPOSITE SEX
develop at
HIS OWN RATE.

[144]

Meanwhile, as we have recognized repeatedly, beneath the surface our adolescent is tremendously concerned with his feelings. He is pulling back from them, uncertain. He wants to like himself. He wants others to like him. He doesn't want to show or do what he believes is "bad." And yet the urges in him are strong.

Inside him expectation is warring with hesitance and hope is arguing with fear.

In some way, somehow, his body feelings must be managed.

He would like to ask: What can I do with these feelings? How can I control them without crushing them out? Please, can't you help me find some way that's safe and lets me feel I'm all right?

If we are to help him, we must keep in mind what we know well at this point—that even though the strength of his urgency is stepped up, the sex feelings themselves are not new.

Far earlier, in all probability, he found a way of gratifying the body feelings through touching himself.

With the unfolding interest in sex and the fresh wave of feelings accompanying physical development, the boy or girl usually starts masturbating once again or continues it with a stronger and more irresistible urge. Then, if old feelings of shame and guilt persist, as they many times do, the increased urgency makes for greater conflict.

He tries to stop.

He can't.

He struggles in vain. Inside himself he suffers untold agonies. He feels himself a horrible failure. He can't like himself. How can anyone like him?

The misery of self-condemnation makes fear heavier in him. It makes him feel more than ever that he is "bad." He deserves to be punished or hurt.

[145]

And so he is all set to believe anew any old "horror" stories about masturbation that reach his ears from the outside or that echo inside from his "forgotten" past.

On a sound scientific basis we can say masturbation in itself does not mar body or mind. We can say that many boys and many girls do it. And that it hurts neither. It does not make a girl frigid. It does not make her less capable of enjoying sex when she marries. Nor does it make a man impotent. It does not drain his sap or waste his seed. There are millions of sperm cells in the testicles and new millions are constantly being generated.

"Like in a factory!" one teen-ager exclaimed in relief.

Asked Carl, another teen-ager, full of worry, "Are you quite certain Pop, it won't make you crazy?"

"No, it won't. That's a stupid old superstition."

The belief arose out of what doctors and attendants noticed in institutions for the mentally ill. People who are insane do often lose inhibitions. They lose their sense of time and place and do many things openly which ordinarily would be confined to privacy. This Carl's father made clear to his son.

Time and time again, a boy or girl feels that others can tell what they have been doing by looking at them.

"Isn't there a certain look about you? Or dark circles? Or a pasty, pimply skin?"

Such things are completely untrue.

So also is another worry that many parents have. "I've heard," said one, "that if a person masturbates, it keeps him solitary. He is apt to find too much satisfaction in it and won't bother then to seek satisfaction in more mature ways."

The person who has within himself emotional conflicts that make him withdraw may use prolonged masturbation well past the time when he could be marrying. If our youngster is a recluse and we know that he masturbates, our concern needs to be directed at removing the solitariness, not at removing the solace. Using the masturbation as solace is the result, not the cause.

The more anxious and insecure a youngster is, the more he needs a solace. The more afraid he is, the more he needs it. Fear that he will be hurt by "giving in" to his sex feelings only adds to this need.

Occasionally a parent feels free enough and convinced enough inside himself to say casually, "It doesn't hurt! Not in any way."

Occasionally a parent can even add, "I was unwise to frighten you by silly warnings when you were little. I know now that that was one of the mistakes I made in bringing you up."

At best, masturbation can only be a substitute. Until the sex drive can permissibly lead to mature contacts and the culmination of love and mating, the problem remains of finding some means of temporarily handling sexual feelings.

Parents who know that the sex drive is strong know also that it will in some fashion have to be released. They know that stifling it and trying to keep it under entirely makes it more difficult to control.

"I've heard that when you play football hard enough, it takes care of the sex instincts," says Rod crestfallenly. "I certainly wish it would."

"They say if you keep your mind on higher things and are real, real busy, you won't have time for sexy thoughts," says Rhoda with equal discouragement.

Some adolescents cannot, other adolescents can and do manage to divert sex feelings into nonsexual channels. It's as if the urge to procreate biologically were transferred to the urge to create in some social or intellectual sphere.

Great and zealous devotion to a cause, especially in a group with others who are similarly devoted, may call forth so much

[147]

creative energy that the sex urge diminishes in its place of importance.

Sometimes quite another thing is true. The fact that the sex urge is attached too strongly to fear may make it necessary to turn to so-called "higher" outlets. Fanaticism of one sort or another may be as much a sign of emotional conflict as is the sowing of wild oats. It is, however, rarely as shocking to parents. For it does not bring social censorship down.

Biological and social creativity do not exclude each other, fortunately, or man would not prosper. A healthy interest in artistic, religious or other modes of expression need not exclude a healthy interest in sex. However, the teen-ager who throws himself with wholehearted enthusiasm into activities ordinarily does discharge enough emotional energy to make the controlling and channeling of the sex urge easier.

This makes good sense.

He needs satisfying achievements, satisfying endeavors, sports and hobbies, outgoing friendly relationships, memberships in groups, taking part in social and religious activities.

Different youngsters will, of course, emphasize different things according to differing dispositions, strivings and tastes.

Different parents will also hold to different emphases and beliefs.

If you happen to be among those parents who feel that they do not want to say anything openly to their children, still if you can accept and understand inside yourself what their true feelings are—this will be all to the good. They will sense your understanding and this will be helpful in and of itself.

TO WAIT OR NOT TO?

Sooner or later, this question comes up.

"You hear so much these days about it, Len," Howard's mother said very seriously to Howard's father. "Howard's been seeing an awful lot of Ina lately. Don't you think you'd better talk to him?"

Howard's father looked thoughtful. "But he's just a kid, Gay. Only seventeen! Aren't you making far too much of it?"

"They start in awfully young, I've gathered. And they get in awfully deep. And some of it's because they have no one to talk things over with."

"We managed all right."

"But don't you remember, darling? We did an awful lot of agonizing."

"Hmmm!" Father looked sober. "And at that we were a good deal older than Howard. You're in, dear, as the expression goes. You have my blessing to go ahead and start with Howard whenever you wish."

"But Len! It's not my job. It's yours. I was okay when he was small. But in his teens a boy needs to talk with a man rather than a woman. If there's no man in the family it's different, of course. However, if you don't want to, we can ask Dr. Nelson if he will, or Pastor Gray. They've both done a lot with young people. I've had discussions with them and they say it's often easier for a son or daughter to talk with an outsider . . ."

"Not our boy!" belligerently. "I want a try first!"

"After all, Howard and I are quite used to talking, man to man. We discuss business and politics and what's in the news. And yet none of those things are as important as this. Only I'll have to count on you, Gay, to give me all the pointers you can from that class you've been going to. And I'd like also to have a couple of up-to-date books."

Even so, when Father opened the subject, he found himself clearing his throat. "I've been wondering, Howard, about you and Ina."

"How do you mean?" with a note of challenge in Howard's voice.

"Hmmm!" thought his father. "He's probably afraid I'm prying into his privacy." And aloud, "I know the two of you like each other a lot and that you have a lot to work out together. I'm not after confidences from you. What you want to tell me is up to you. But I did want to tell you a couple of things that were on *my* mind."

"Now, Pop, please don't lecture. She's a wonderful girl and I'm terribly much in love with her and she likes me too."

Very simply and directly, then, Howard's father went on to say that he knew that sex feelings were a very great problem when people were in their middle and late teens . . .

"You've said it, Dad. I've only got one life and sometimes I wonder if I'll ever get married or if I'll end up in a uniform on the other side of the world."

Father nodded, accepting Howard's feelings. "I know how it is."

"But, Dad," from Howard, suddenly questioning, "I worry a lot too. It's not really so simple. I want to a lot. I love Ina so much. And then I think of all the things that could happen." And after a pause, "I think the biggest worry is if we were to go ahead, I might get Ina pregnant. And then, just suppose I'd have to leave."

"You've got a big point there. You can't belittle it. Because there isn't any method of birth control that's a hundred per cent reliable. You always take a chance.

"And even if you married with our consent and her parents', you'd be shoved into responsibilities long before you were ready or able to take them on. Marriage then would be something you were forced into instead of the thing you wanted most in life."

Father spoke in the tone of a man philosophizing to himself rather than preaching. And since young people in their middle and late teens are themselves great philosophers if given half a chance, this struck a responsive chord.

[150]

"In this life there are a lot of times when you have to settle with partial solutions and make peace within yourself in terms of these. You have to consider the world outside yourself and the world inside yourself as well.

"Because you and Ina are the kind of people who want to have respect from others and who want to have *self-respect* also, to use an old-fashioned term, I have an idea that you'll feel as I do, that it's better to wait."

Glancing at Howard, Father caught the quick gulp and the serious look of determination.

This was all for now. But here, as elsewhere, Howard's father had considered his boy's feelings as well as his acts.

It is not always love, however, that makes a boy or girl "go the limit."

Sexual escapades may, for one thing, be a defiant gesture by the teen-ager. Revolt over our condemnation of his sex feelings may then add itself to revolt over other things about which he is already hostile. He may then take to using *sex as a means of letting his hostility out.*

Says Wilma, sixteen, "I got sick and tired of my parents' lack of understanding. I got sick and tired of their constant blame. I know if they knew what I've done, it would hurt them. Maybe," protesting angrily, "maybe I should feel terrible. But I don't."

Underneath the surface, however, Wilma did. For entering into a sex act with one person in order to hurt another person has little to do with love. Obviously it cannot bring security. It can bring only an increased sense of guilt.

Another reason why an adolescent "goes the limit" is to find a closeness and a confirmation he feels he has lacked. In this case what he is seeking, however, is rarely companionship or mutuality. In his mind he pastes a parent picture onto the partner and goes to him with dependence, trying to get him to be an imagined substitute parent who will give him the acceptance he feels his real parents haven't. Most of all he wants acceptance for the sexual impulses which he believes his parents have refused to countenance.

His dilemma is clear.

After all, the person he has turned to is *not* a parent. Factually the adolescent is still dependent on his real parents because of his age if for no other reason. And so when he returns to them after his escapade, he comes feeling anxious and miserably apologetic in spite of his attempts to deny this. He fears that they may find out and condemn him—perhaps even discard him. Whatever security he had with them before is lessened now by the worry that floods within.

Some boys and girls try to gain a sense of achievement and prowess through sexual exploits. Some try through daring to prove that their fears of being hurt and punished are unfounded.

But these efforts usually fail.

Even where the love motive prevails, anxiety enters.

The adolescent who has intercourse before he is emotionally ready for a steady, steadfast relationship ordinarily is torn. It is practically impossible to grow up in our present culture without acquiring hesitance and doubt.

And so, as parents we do well to take a firm stand: *"It's better for you to wait to have intercourse until you are old enough to marry. And it's best to be married before you do."*

Here are some of the reasons:

> Sexual compatibility is important in marriage. Because of feelings we do not fully comprehend, it often takes a while to work out a sexual relationship so that it is satisfying. Full, mutual enjoyment may not be reached for a period of time.

"You mean we may not like sex together right away?" asked down-to-earth, frank young Harriet. "It may take us a while to get used to each other? Perhaps we'll be discouraged at moments meanwhile. And if we're not married, I, for one, would be scared to death that John might get tired of me and leave."

To enjoy sex fully, one must be able to be oneself fully. One must be able to be free and vital in many aspects of the mutual relationship. But where fear of desertion enters, constriction enters also. And this ties a person up and defeats sexual adjustment.

"You mean I've got to be free enough to be myself—to get mad, for instance, when I feel mad at John, and that I need to be able to take it too when he gets moody." And yet not be afraid that he'll run away."

"That's about it. Ordinarily you can work it out better when you know you're assured of being together, not having to worry whether one or the other in an angry or discouraged moment will call it quits."

Among the conditions that facilitate compatibility is the intimate tie of living and working together. Sharing a home and mutual endeavors backed by the feel of steadiness that comes with marriage—this is more conducive to sexual adjustment than the fly-by-night arrangements. For the latter cause anxiety and unrest to enter during a time in which making adaptation to one another calls for stability and peace.

One mother exclaimed, "At last I can see things clearly. These young ones want their parents to ADMIT IT'S ALL RIGHT FOR THEM TO HAVE GOOD FEELINGS and at one and the same time to HELP THEM CONTROL THEIR ACTS."

As with other feelings, sexual feelings need to be channeled.

[153]

If an adolescent can feel assured that his overwhelming desire to masturbate is harmless, then his anxiety may diminish. He may then feel less driven into acts which he would regret and more certain of being able to control his impulses. He can wait far more securely until he is grown.

Once more it boils down to the same old principle:

It's important to find
HEALTHY OUTLETS FOR FEELINGS
at the same time that you
GUIDE AND CONTROL THE ACTS.

A wholesome, active, doing life. A vital philosophy. Ideals that have been acquired by "absorption," as it were, over the long years. And a hearty admission that sex feelings are normal. All these stand the teen-ager in good stead.

A WORD ABOUT SEX WITH THE SAME SEX

Just as some adolescents get into sexual escapades in a mistaken effort to solve their problems, so do some turn away from sexual expression. Because of the shame and guilt inside them, they may try for one thing to keep sex out of their lives entirely. Or they may turn to members of the same sex to accept them with their sexual needs.

In the preadolescent period and in early adolescence, hero worship and crushes and adherence to friendships with members of the same sex are, as we know, quite in order. They seem to help a boy or girl make the transition from attachments to members of his own family to attachments outside his home.

Most children before adolescence at some time or another have had open sex play with children of the same sex. This is a far more common occurrence than most parents suspect and need not be taken as alarming. It is much as though two little like-sexed dogs were playing around with each other. Unless

[154]

too much guilt or anxiety has built up, it ordinarily passes without having done any permanent harm.

Some boys and girls, as we've seen, may be slow in developing an interest in the opposite sex. They may be slow in their all-round maturing.

In general, the boy or girl who matures sooner physically will mature sooner socially and emotionally as well, and will evidence interest sooner than does the boy or girl who matures later.

Some boys may turn temporarily with the upsurge of sex feelings at this age to sexual experimentation with other boys. Some girls with other girls. If they are isolated from contacts with the opposite sex, this can readily happen. When contacts become more accessible, then boy-girl attractions are resumed. Keeping away any actual social or physical barriers to being with members of the opposite sex is therefore enormously important all through the adolescent years.

Timidity and hesitance about one's own attractiveness and worth-whileness may set up barriers to free-flowing contacts as surely as high walls or locked doors. Guilt and shame over one's body sensations add to timidity and a feeling of worthlessness. Relieving these may relieve the sense of blight that keeps a youngster apart from the opposite sex.

Parental disapproval and warnings, on the other hand, can fortify hesitance.

Take Winifred, for example. When she was fourteen, her mother said, beaming, "She's such a good, wholesome girl, my Winifred. Thank goodness she's not the type to go for lipstick or boys."

Two years went by without new developments. Winifred's mother looked seriously thoughtful. "Maybe," she apologized, "maybe my girl's a little slow."

Two years later, however, with the worry lines between her brows, she showed real concern. "Can't you please tell me

[155]

what's wrong with Winifred? She's eighteen and she still scorns the make-up that the other girls around her wear. And I don't believe she knows that boys exist."

Then, with voice dropping, she brought out her great fear. "I've heard so much about homosexuality. If Winifred had any very good girl friends I'd be scared out of my wits. I guess I am anyway, because I understand that a person can have homosexual tendencies without these being openly expressed. Do you suppose they're what Winifred's got?"

Winifred's mother had heard or read that homosexuality could be expressed in open sex practices with members of the same sex. She had also come across the term "latent homosexuality," which means that so much of the person's emotions stay focused on the same sex that not enough of the sex urge is free to attach itself to members of the opposite sex. When development of sexual interests does not appear normally, this sort of halting of emotional development may be playing its part.

Homosexuality is not a physical abnormality. A person is not born with it. Various things may lie at the bottom of it, as, for instance, an exaggerated fear of making relationships with members of the opposite sex and fear fantasies that have become so intense as to halt emotional growth.

Trying to push the boy or girl into boy-girl contacts does little good. Trying to control the matter by lecturing, by threats or by punishment is not effective either. The problem is too complex and complicated. So is that of extreme solitariness or of "wildness." One is neither "worse" nor "better" than the others. They all show disturbances calling for help more skilled and impersonal than the parent is equipped to give.

As far as Winifred was concerned, it did not matter whether there was so-called "homosexuality" or some other basis for her difficulty. The natural interest which she should have had in boys was, for some reason, not in functioning order. This called for professional help just as do escapades which have gone too far. For the person who is trained to understand the language of the unconscious can help the child better to get at the hidden causes and release the fears and emotional disturbances which have either been holding him back or driving him on.*

Meanwhile, let us move from these more serious problems to the everyday problems that you, as parents, want to be able to handle yourselves. Let us turn to boy-girl contacts—our major concern—and consider some of the very practical matters related to how your child *acts* in his early and middle teens. Let's look at some specific points about "dating" rules for him and at questions about you which may help to determine his response.

Let us ask:

HOW DO YOU RATE IN REGARD TO YOUR YOUNGSTER'S DATES?

We know that the teen-ager wants and needs the protection of sound rules and regulations to help him control his acts. They bring him the certainty he must have in the face of his own uncertainty until he grows into more mature sureness.

With some boys and girls *dependable independence* comes earlier than with others. But until it is present, a teen-ager wants your rules. They are enormously important props even though he may resist them.

The respect which you have paid to his feelings will be a large factor in determining the respect he pays to your rules.

The assurance which you feel in regard to what you request will also be important.

What rules are drawn up will depend on your own convic-

* See also page 186 about professional resources.

tions, your background, the customs of the families with whom you associate. It will depend too on what you learn about the customs and rules among the friends with whom your teen-ager goes.

Do you know about his crowd's dating customs?

Discuss these with him. Find out what his crowd does.

Don't forget, however, that his fantasies may color his reports. What he states may more nearly approximate conditions as he wants them to exist rather than as they do actually exist.

"Susy doesn't have to stay home week nights," Florence reports to her parents. "Florence doesn't have to stay home week nights" Susy reports to hers, adding "You shouldn't keep pressuring me to stay home . . ." "So?" we might ask. "Who's pressuring whom?"

You will not want your child to be too different. And yet on some scores you will need to insist on differences.

About times to go out and the time to come home

"Two nights during the school week are enough for dating. Short dates only. Earlier to bed is a must!!"

"No, Ellen, even though the other girls don't have to be in at any special time, we don't think it's wise for a sixteen-year-old to be out till three or four in the morning. Let's settle on a more reasonable time and stick with it . . ."

"But, Mother, suppose we get into a traffic jam on the way home? Or that all the rest of the kids go for a snack? How can you expect me to get in on the dot of the minute hand?"

"I won't. We'll grant half an hour's leeway . . ."

"And if it's a party, of course I'll just have to stay till the end."

"That's right. Making you leave early wouldn't be fair. So we'll want to know when you go to a real party and where."

"Since we care with whom and where—"

"We'd like to know in general where you're going. To a movie. To a dance or what . . ."

"We may be old-fashioned but we want to meet your boy friends. We don't believe in this horn-blowing routine. When Tom comes for you next time, please invite him in . . ."

"Double dates, yes; single dates, no. Not for the present . . ."

"You said Judd asked you up to his apartment? I'm glad you told me. No, I don't think it's wise."

Do you meet her dates with grace?

When daughter brings her boy friend in, do you, her mother, in an attempt to be charming, give her a feeling that you may be trying to outshine her? Or do you, her father, in your attempt to be a hail fellow, really shove your girl into a back seat?

Don't be a holder-onto or a prier-into. Neither one helps.

Are you a night watchman waiting up for your youngster's return?

"For heaven's sake, Mother, go to bed!"

Are your punishments too punishing?

"Imagine! They made me call off the big party. I'd been looking forward to it for weeks. That was to teach me! To teach me what? How to be meaner than mean to get even! . . . Anyway I felt they'd turned against me. So I put on my jeans and I took my toothbrush and nightgown and I got on the bus and went to my friend's . . ."

Do you yourself remember the agony of punishments that brought humiliation? They're never worth it, no matter what the crime. If you do deny privileges, at least don't make the

[159]

denials cover conspicuous times. And do permit your adolescent "outs" that save face.

Do you practice protective interference?

Do you, for instance, keep young brothers away?

Are you dependable about the car?

You promised he could have it. And then you decided to go out the same night. It might just as well have been the next night because it was just one of those "when-can-we-make-it" affairs.

That's one thing.

But it's another when you already have a date and a relatively unimportant one comes up for him and he starts to beg and you begin to feel "cruel." Do you stick with your conviction anyway that it's right to consider yourself rather than martyr yourself? If you do the latter, resentment is bound to follow and you'll take it out on him in some way no doubt.

How sympathetic are you in those pathetic "crises"?

When she's been starry-eyed, expecting a blind date to be her big moment and he turns out a "flop" . . .

When status and prestige are deflated by a lack of a Saturday night date . . .

When he's turned down or she's stood up . . .

These are awful moments, not to be belittled in their crushing weight.

How is your party behavior?

"My parents! They make pretenses to come downstairs and check. Imagine! My mother came down last night to see if I was burning myself with a *fork!!!*"

On the other hand . . . "My parents are wonderful! Do you know what they've done? They say young people need independence. So, because our place is small, they fixed up their room so it could be a sitting room, not only a bedroom. Now they're out of the way and comfortable there after the introductions are over when I have my friends in. And they're on hand if I need them, which gives me a feeling that's mighty good . . ."

Remember: There are few absolute rules. Most of them should be reviewed in relation to you, to your child and to the resolution that you can come to in terms of your standards and his standards—always, however, adhering to the standards of health, of safety, and of necessary legal demands.

Sometimes it is possible to make things happier all round if the parents of the boys and girls who go together can comfortably manage to get together.

It happened that Randy went with a group whose parents lived in one neighborhood. Randy's mother was an enterprising and friendly soul. She invited various mothers to tea in the afternoons, some of the fathers and mothers over for after-dinner coffee. What could be more natural under these circumstances than that the talk drift to parents and children?

"I think if we could have some common agreement about what our respective children should and shouldn't do, it would be more comfortable for all of them."

"And for us!"

"A good idea, Mrs. Jones."

Even so, our youngsters are bound on occasion to protest what we ask. They wouldn't be normal if they didn't.

"I know you think we're old fogies," one father commented, accepting his daughter's feelings, "or old bags, or whatever you call it . . . We are interested, though, in whatever arguments you have. We want to hear them." Thus he provided an action outlet for the feelings of protest. He knew that if revolt and hostility were there it was better to have them come out directly in face-to-face discussion than to have them store up and come out away from home, behind his back.

A few major "don'ts" are important for us too in connection with the "don'ts" that we level at our adolescents.

Don't have too many "don'ts" at a time.

Don't have too many unnecessary "don'ts" (although you will doubtless have some that you consider necessary and that your child is sure are not).

Don't make rules that you know will only be broken. It's no use, for instance, to forbid necking. You know your youngster will neck after he's reached a stage of bolder interest boy-girl-wise. Don't forbid him to talk about sex with other youngsters. He probably will talk about it anyway. Most youngsters do. It serves as a safety valve for letting out feelings that might otherwise take a more hazardous path.

Check yourself frequently:

Do you approve or disapprove when your young one starts going with members of the opposite sex? Are you suspicious or fearful? Do you hold the reins so tight that he wants to break free of them? Are your reins so loose that he misses their steadying effect?

These are hard questions to answer. How you handle the day-by-day details of your teen-ager's dating activities is one way in which you express to him what he can expect of you. How you feel is another. He'll learn from both.

And the repeat of two more important DO's for you:

Whenever possible talk things over first instead of dictating without discussion. You may need to dictate in the end. But

[162]

meanwhile the talking will have given your boy or girl a chance to get out his feelings and thoughts.

And: Remember that whether you voice it or not, it's important for you to be able to admit to yourself that he has sex urges which are important to him. Try to bear with him. For one of his great tasks during these years is to find peace with himself on their score.

AND SOME WORDS TO REMIND YOU

As you have read these pages on sex education, you have no doubt come to see that sex education is broad and complex. Perhaps at this moment you are therefore wishing for some pointers to summarize a few of the things you can do . . .

Remember—

In the matter of sex education, probably more than in any other, you're bound to have made mistakes. Own up to them. Admit that you've made them. To yourself admit them for certain. And if you feel like it, admit them to your teen-ager, too.

Keep in mind that good body feelings are permissible. And that there are safe and harmless ways of finding at least temporary, partial gratifications.

Recognize that your child is bound to feel hostile toward you for the fact that you have not been able to meet all the curiosities and questions and sex wishes he has had. You couldn't have. It's impossible. Even so, if you let him get his hostility out for the present and past lacks he has felt, even though some of these are imagined, it will help prevent him from using sex as an indirect way of letting hostility out.

Don't be afraid to set limits and to define what he may and may not *do*.

If, like many youngsters, he doesn't bring up the subject of sex, you do it if you can.

[163]

If you feel embarrassed in doing it, say so.

If he wants to talk, listen to him. If he happens to bring in old fears and childish beliefs, don't make fun of them. Many strange, childish fantasies are commonly held over. Truths often sink in better after fantasies have been expressed.

If you like, it won't hurt, and it may help, to mention some of the child fantasies you now know are common.* Tell them much as you would tell a folk tale or story. "Children often imagine—thus and so!" After all, these are childish folk tales that most of our children once told themselves. With the re-telling a teen-ager may now be able to sever the connections between fact and fiction that he put together when he was small. But don't pry for old memories. That only does harm.

What he needs now is for us to take his love affairs seriously, which does not, however, mean somberly. We can smile with him but not laugh at him. He wants us to listen to how he feels and to be glad he is telling us. He resents reactions like those of Deborah's parents.

Sobbed fifteen-year-old Deborah, flouncing out of the living room, "You're horrible, you two! Forbidding me to marry Kent when I grow up. I don't care if he isn't socially suitable. I'm going to marry him, I tell you, whether you disapprove or not."

What these teen-agers crave is to have their feelings accepted with reactions similar to those that Edith's folks gave. Although Edith, too, was only fifteen, they listened with serious interest. "He's simply super, let's face it! I don't see how such a wonderful fellow even wants to *look* at me. We've got so many plans. He's going to study eventually to be a doctor. It doesn't matter how many years it takes. We'll get married as soon as we're old enough and I'll train for a secretarial job or to be an actress, I can't decide quite which. I'd rather be an actress, of course. But then the theater is so demanding. We'd

* See Chapter 8.

[164]

never be together in the evening and that wouldn't work. I expect I'll have an awful job learning shorthand. I haven't that kind of a mind. But you can do anything, almost, for love."

"And it gives you a wonderful feeling," Mother put in, "to dream and plan."

"Only sometimes it's so frustrating because there's such a long stretch to go."

"Yes, I know."

Remember—

These youngsters hope so mightily for our understanding. They want us to respect the fact that they are involved emotionally as deeply as they dare. This affair may last. It may not. Most boys and girls go through several heart-shattering relationships in the process of maturing. They are trying out their fledgling wings, as it were, feeling out what it is like to be a man or a woman in love.* In this process they are enormously grateful for our steady and dignified regard.

Remember—

These boys and girls are struggling to have their love needs and sex needs met at a period in life when they possess bodies that are old enough for complete satisfactions which must, however, be curtailed in a world that says "Wait."

And: Remember this also—

CONTROLLING SEX HAS MORE TO IT THAN SEX

As we have seen very clearly by now, the sexual urges in adolescence are important for many and diverse reasons. Their propelling drive is not only biological. It is emotional, too. Behind it may lie not only the push for sexual outlets but also

* See Chapter 15.

other emotional forces. The push for hostile outlets, for instance. The struggle to satisfy a too-little-satisfied sense of achievement, to prove one is liked when one feels one isn't and to gain comforting closeness one feels one lacks. The desperate necessity to decry and deny fear. The pathetic wish to be liked and to have one's "bad" parts accepted, and the deep and pervading need to like oneself.

We know now this is true:

> The teen-ager uses sex
> not only
> TO SATISFY SEX IMPULSES.
> He may turn to sex
> TO SATISFY OTHER IMPULSES
> as well.

Therefore, to help him control his sexual impulses, we need to consider many things in addition to sex . . .

It's rounding a circle. It takes us back to helping him gain varied satisfactions in the whole of his life.

PART THREE: TOWARD GROWING INDEPENDENCE

11. The Little Matter of Big Responsibilities

MUST HOUSEHOLD CHORES BE BORES
OR BONES OF CONTENTION?

"You want the privileges of this house," scolds Morton's mother. "All right. But for goodness' sake, take some of the responsibilities. Just look at that lawn. It's like a hayfield! And today the garbage man came on his rounds. But no, the can wasn't out on the curb. If mowing the lawn and carrying out the garbage isn't little enough to ask, I'll ask you . . ."

Morton yanked at his hair and gnashed his teeth in a kind of desperation. "Gee, Mother. That's just it. You never *ask* me. You *tell* me. You sit 'way up there on a heavenly cloud or something and hand down orders about what little Mortie *has* to do. Only I'm not little Mortie any more. I've got a mind of my own and I'd like to use it."

"Then why don't you remember the lawn and the garbage?"

"Because," said Morton, suddenly calm, "I don't remember *because* I want to forget."

The same truth holds for many teen-agers. When they are summarily commanded to do things, they are apt to revolt. And the simplest way of rebelling is to forget.

"That sweet smirk that Esther puts on"—Esther's mother

grimaces—"and her everlasting apologies! 'I'm so sorry, Mother darling! It completely slipped my mind!!' . . . I could tar and feather her; I could."

Says Fred, "My folks say I should take responsibility. But if you ask me I'm a slave-labor expert. A yes man. A pair of hands, no less, for the dame who takes all the responsibility into her own hands and bosses the show."

Fred feels like a nobody in his home.

In contrast, in their home the twins, Dan and Diane, each feels like somebody. They take a part and a very active one. They are not conscripted into it. Their chores are not assigned arbitrarily. They are given a voice and a choice.

However, it had not always been so.

The big change came after the talk which had started between Father and Mother and which then had spread to include the twins.

"We've gone about this thing all wrong, Del," then father had announced to their mother one evening. "No wonder those kids keep crawling out from under. We've given them the feeling that all we wanted them to do was what we ourselves didn't want to do."

"Well, it's true, isn't it?"

"True, but not good. I read a book that started me thinking and I believe I've come up with something: This is your home and my home. And each of us can get the best out of having a home only as we put ourselves into making a home."

"You're a wonderful man, dear," Del smiled. "My father never talked that way to my mother. He said, 'It's your job, Ma.' And he sat on the side lines, not as cheerleader but as chief Mr. Big Complainer. And my mother, of course, acted the martyr and drafted us to lessen her horrible burden instead of to help in the fun of making and keeping a home."

"Nice philosophy you've got there, Del. But if I remember correctly, it's not all a bed of roses. How about that mess of a stopped-up sink I fixed last week and the mess of clothes you had to wash as result? And how about those times when you're tired and complain so bitterly?"

"Why," with a twinkle, "that's part of the fun. I have as much right to complain as my mother had, haven't I? . . . A fine ambition! . . . Well, anyhow, let's go."

So they called in Dan and Diane. And they talked about three things:

WHAT—

HOW—

WHEN—

What jobs needed doing and what each might do to take part in running the home. As far as possible Dan and Diane made their own choices. Dan wanted to polish the floors, for one thing, with the new electric waxer. And he elected the job of washing the windows. Diane volunteered, "I'd like to take on the family mending, not just my own. And," unexpectedly, "I'd like to dish-wash. I love the feel of the suds."

"Hm!" thought Father, his mind harking back to earlier protests. "But I guess when it's a self-chosen task it's different!" Nonetheless he held his peace and listened as Diane continued to name the jobs she preferred. "Gee, Dad," he heard her asking, "do you suppose I could help you wash the car?"

When the choices were exhausted there were still some tedious chores hanging in air. "Let's be fair about them," Diane put in. "Let's divide them up evenly. Mother, you decide."

Meanwhile Dan had taken notes and came in with the suggestion that the various jobs be posted. "I'll make a bulletin board," he volunteered.

"Fine," said Father. "And if things don't work out well as planned, if we strike any humps, let's call for a conference to iron them out. In any case, in a month let's get together for

[171]

further planning and for shifts, if we wish, in our particular jobs."

So much for deciding on *what* each one would do.

Next came some considerations of *how* the various jobs were to be done. Most important: By whose standards would they be judged?

They talked about jobs in general. If Dan were accepting a job, for instance, outside of the home, he would have to meet certain requirements. He would have to be responsible to a boss or supervisor. Here at home, Mother would supervise certain things, Father would supervise others. Certain standards of performance would be judged by them.

As for the method of doing the job, however, that was up to the person doing it. "You mean it?" Diane exclaimed. "You mean you're going to let me dry the dishes *my* way? The way we've learned in our homemaking class is the most sanitary? Rinse and stand. No dirty dish towels? . . . Boy, that's a victory!"

They talked, too, about the fact that in every job situation disagreeable moments are apt to arise. Parts of the job become tedious.

"Then I'll get sore that I chose it."

"Of course you will."

"And I'll gripe."

"Of course."

As to the *when's,* this too came in for discussion. Leaving dishes till next morning was out since Mother would need the sink counter early to pack lunches for the day. Wash would need to be done before the supply was exhausted. Watering the garden would need to be done when best for the plants. Beds would need to be made up in the morning—to save Mother's "nerves."

They talked, too, about the fact that there would be times when it would be necessary for some one to take over another's job. "Don't just duck out. Let us know if you've got orchestra practice after school, or if you want time to get a dress hemmed. We can arrange to substitute for you on occasion, of course."

It was this very dropping of insistence on rigidly enforced regularity that seemed to bring the greatest sense of ease. As time passed it cemented accord and kept the spirit of cooperation going.

There are some occasions, obviously, when parents must ask a boy or girl to take over a job regardless of choice.

"Mother's sick, John. Grandma can come over, but she can't stay after four. So we'll need you at home then to answer the telephone and the door and to keep an eye on Janey till I get home at six," said John's father.

Even though it meant that John would miss his afternoon ball game with the boys, this job had to take precedence. Since it was an emergency and also a situation which was not abused in their family, John agreed with good will.

We parents need to remember that children do have their own jobs to do. Going to school, getting lessons done, these are most important jobs. Taking part in school club activities and being with their peers—these too are of the utmost importance. The jobs at home naturally fall into a secondary classification in the minds of these youngsters. When they acquire homes of their very own, things will be different. Then their sense of the job's importance will undergo a material change.

Right now they want and need to have home be a place in which to relax, not only a place in which to work. The lazy and leisurely moments of letting down and of doing nothing in particular may add far more to a child's feeling that home is home than any amount of work participation. The ideal thing is to find a balance between the two. But no family can always achieve the ideal. And sometimes "easy come" is a better policy than to keep forcing and pushing "cooperation."

After all, true cooperation cannot be commandeered. You can demand that a job be done. But you cannot demand that the spirit follow the flesh. You can work at getting a youngster's cooperation and nurture and cherish what you get. But in the last analysis, it is his to give and he will give it only as he feels like giving.

Letting our boys and girls have a say in *what* to do and *how* and *when* to do it may prove helpful. Permitting them their gripes when they feel like griping may make for the more willing spirit when the griping is temporarily over. Giving them chances for creative endeavors in the home as well as—or even instead of—the regular chores may in the long run bring greater reward.

PUTTING THAT CREATIVE URGE TO USE IN THE HOME

"You should see Marie's room," groans her mother. "It's a horror. But it was such a dream room to start. Those pink organdie curtains! And that adorable pink and white rug! And the white wallpaper with the pink rosebuds on it. The most girly-girl room I ever saw! At least it *was*. But now it's not pink and white. It's one solid gray smudge. And to think of the hours I put into decorating it. It's the kind of room I was always mad to have in my teens."

But unfortunately it was not what Marie had been mad to have.

Sandra's mother was wiser. "Your room needs doing over, Sandy. We've got so-and-so much to spend. What would you like to do with it?"

"Oh, Mother." Sandra's dark eyes glistened. "I'd like it real sexy and modern. Green and mole gray with splashes of watermelon. I can just see it. It'll be so becoming to me and my coloring."

And three and five and ten months later, "Don't you love it, Jane?" to a new friend. "Isn't it divine?" to another. "Keep your cruddy hands off my bedcover," to young brother. "Don't you dare track mud in there," to the brother next in line.

Complains Ida's mother, "My girl will never help in the kitchen. You'd think she'd like to give me a hand."

But from Ida, "Why should I? Nothing I do is ever right. 'Drain the lettuce. No, not in that sieve, in this. Mash the potatoes. No, not through the ricer; take the wooden bowl. Be careful now not to set the oven too high. Be sure now not to pour the batter too soon.' . . . I go nuts."

In Milly and Milt's home a different kind of kitchen deal is in operation. "We take different nights, each of us, to get the dinner. Or sometimes we double up," Milly explains the system. "We do the planning and the shopping and the cooking and serving. Whoever's in charge is really in charge, within budgeting limits, of course. On my night last week I tried a Chinese dinner. One of the girls in my social studies class who is Chinese took me down to her father's store and he explained to me just what to get and how to cook things. Milt is less of an experimentalist. We always know that on his night we can count on hot dogs or hamburgers. My mother's good! She surprises us with new things. But it's my father who takes the prize. He's the best! Sometimes he lets me help him and I learn a lot."

It wasn't long after that Milt proposed to his mother that on her day as well as on his he might relieve her by doing the shopping. "It'll save you lots of time, Ma. And I'm learning to watch for bargain ads. So if you give me your order list a few days ahead I think I can cut down some of the expenses for you."

Judd wanted a chance for creativity in the garden outside. He planned and planted a rock garden which he cultivated and added to bit by bit. This did not, however, keep his father from lending a helping hand. There was no fuming, "It's yours and you take care of it." There was, rather, the willingness to cooperate which engendered return willingness. "You're going to the track meet this Saturday, Judd? Want me to go over your end of the yard while I'm working on mine?"

Creativity in the home need not, however, function only in big, long-term projects. The making of a lamp shade. The baking of a cake. The sewing of a curtain. The tinting of an old, faded bedspread in colors especially mixed to suit one's own mind and eye. Arranging two curving branches in a brass bowl. Singing three songs of one's own gay choice on a foggy evening. Building a tray rack. Setting the table with contrasting mats and napkins instead of the ones that came together. Many things that are little as well as those that are big.

Whether or not a youngster cooperates or enters into creative home activities depends to some extent on his age and interests. As we have seen, there are so many other things to intrigue him, so many other endeavors that consume his hours and his energy. However, his role in the home depends also on his mother's and father's feelings and attitudes.

"My girl won't help," complains Josephine's mother. "And yet she's a better cook than I am. She mends her father's shirts better, too, and can turn his cuffs like an expert . . ." And then, after a thoughtful pause, "A funny thing just crossed my mind. I'm not really pleased. I guess I'm jealous. I want her to understudy me but not to overshadow me. Perhaps she feels my attitude. That may account for her running out."

"My boy won't help!"

A pertinent question here is: Will his dad?

Why should a boy want to help if his father feels that what needs to be done is a woman's job?

In homes where creativity and cooperation exist, certain truths usually pervade the scene. Mother is not the maid of all work. Nor is she the untrusting mistress who must do everything herself to prove it well done. There is no set of rules as to what is conventionally right for old and young or for male and female. The best men can be cooks and the best cooks can be men. Fathers do tend babies. So do older brothers if they can and would like to. Women can till the soil and may want to paint and hammer. Each may bring his own contribution according to his wish and his bent.

SHALL WE PAY HIM FOR JOBS HE DOES AROUND THE HOUSE?

You may ask, as do other parents, whether paying boys and girls for jobs in the home may not prove a useful inducement in furthering cooperation.

Actually several problems are contained in this question. One problem deals with jobs that you would not "hire out."

If a boy or girl undertakes a job that falls into this category of home jobs that you would otherwise do yourself and would not pay anyone to do, then he should not be paid to do them. His cooperating remains cooperative only so long as he does such jobs freely and "for free"—in order to participate, not in order to be paid. Paying for cooperation begets not cooperation but a pseudo giving which is not a gift.

On the other hand, if the job is a job that you would in any case be paying someone to do, then it becomes a different matter. If your teen-ager wishes to apply for it, as it were, and if you believe he can efficiently do what is required, he may well be granted a trial.

Says Lester's father, "I've got to look for another yardman. Old Mack gave notice today."

"Could I have a try at it?" Lester asks.

So Father and Lester line up the requirements. What needs to be done, the standards that must be met, and the specified hours when the help is needed in order to continue the supervision Father used to give Mack.

[177]

As for rate of pay, "If you do the work efficiently, Lester, I'll pay you, of course, what I paid Mack when he started and what I was counting on paying another man at the start."

"Gee, Dad!" grins Lester. "I'll do my darnedest. That's sure different from Wren's dad. Wren was burnt up. His dad offered him thirty-five cents an hour, but then he took on an outside man and paid him a dollar."

"If you're not worth what I'd pay a good man, I won't keep you on any more than I'd keep on another man if he did a sloppy job."

"Yes, Dad, that's fair!"

By the same token, if he wishes to discontinue the job, he must be free to quit with proper notice, just as another employee would be.

"I've enjoyed baby-sitting, Mother, and the money I've earned has been useful. But now that I'm going steady with Bob, I'd like to resign."

"Can you stick it out, dear, till I can find someone else?"

"But of course."

If your youngster took a clerk's job in a store, a packer's job in a delivery room, a loading job on a truck, the same conditions would prevail. He is no longer a child pretending that he has earned the money his father gives him and fantasying that five cents is as big as a dollar or more. The matter of earning money now is more down to earth to him, more practical and real. He, himself, is now earning money as himself, not as an imitated or "play" daddy or mother. His worth and identity should therefore be maintained wherever possible by whoever employs him. For these are values he is striving as an adolescent to attain.

Occasionally circumstances arise where it is not possible to pay the prevailing wage rate but where you want if possible to obtain help at a lesser cost.

Paul's father, for instance, wanted the floor painted, but did not have the time to do it himself. So he asked his boy if he would do it for him. He told him he wanted to pay something but couldn't go high enough to take on a regular worker. Quite frankly he told Paul what he could afford to pay, and quite frankly Paul decided whether he could afford to take on the job.

This was quite different from what Wren's father had done. Wren's father had offered Wren less simply because he was offering it to a son rather than to an outside man, as if Wren's services were worth less. Paul's father, however, made it quite clear that his son's services were worth as much as he could pay anyone. Wren's father devalued, whereas Paul's valued fully what his boy did.

A WORD ON HIS CHOOSING FRIENDS

When a home is a creative home it belongs to everyone in it and everyone in it *belongs.* The sense of belongingness that each feels in it seems to reach out in inviting fashion. Friends seem to feel it and to feel at home in it.

"Come on over, John. I'm cooking the dinner tonight and you can help," says young Milt. "We'll stop and do the shopping on the way."

"Your ma and pop going to be out?"

"No, we're all home."

"You mean you get a chance to go in the kitchen without your ma saying 'Run'? Boy! That's fun."

Many parents complain that they never get to know their children's friends. One reason may be that home is too uneasy a place for friends to be easy in. When home becomes more a place where one can let down and be oneself, this state of affairs may be remedied.

Even so, there are other things which may work against our girls and boys wanting their mothers and fathers to know their companions.

[179]

Communication's the thing!

For one thing, our standards in the choice of friends may interfere with their feeling of being able to choose their own friends according to their lights and desires.

This does not mean that they will not in some instances enjoy the companionship of the sons and daughters of our friends. They may. They may not.

"Our dads went to school together," says Jock with great pride when he introduces his friend James. On the other hand, Florence sniffs, "You like their mothers, I know, Mum. But, honestly, those girls are so affected! I can't stand them. And I don't see why your going with their mothers has to mean that I have to go with them."

In a parents' group, one mother complained, "I can't stand the kind of friends Bruce is forever dragging in . . . Nor can I understand why. They're nice enough boys. *But . . .*" She paused, hesitant.

"But what?" another mother asked her.

"I don't know. It's just that they're so different from the boys I'd pick out for him to be friends with."

"Have you picked out some in particular?"

"Yes. There's the McMaster boy, for instance; he's the same age and just wonderful! I know Mrs. McMaster from the club I go to. The McMasters, you know, they live in that big white house with the gorgeous trees and that great stretch of lawn in front of it. The big house with the regal-looking columns . . ."

Several mothers smiled knowingly and Bruce's mother gasped, "My goodness, what am I saying? I didn't know I was such a social snob! I'm ashamed . . . But," more thoughtfully, "I guess there are reasons. My own reasons that go back to when I was a youngster."

There were.

As a child this woman had always felt "less good." "Less good" than the other girls. Inferior somehow, even though she

[181]

had no actual reason to feel this. She knew from her school achievement that she wasn't intellectually inferior and many times she'd been told she was pretty. "And yet," she mused, "I've always had that feeling. As if I were less attractive than somebody. Somebody very attractive . . ." She paused, squinting her eyes as if trying to get a picture. And then, all of a sudden, the light came flooding. "Of course! My mother! She always came first. First with my father. And I guess as a small girl I wanted to come first. I remember that too."

Like all small girls, this girl had wanted to be more important with her daddy. And because Mother was more important, she had felt herself inferior.

"I've tried one way and another to make up for that feeling. And now I'm trying to make up for it through having Bruce bring home the sort of friends that will build me up. How foolish can you be?"

"But how natural!"

"Isn't it true?"

Being able to choose their own friends is important to our boys and girls. It brings them a sense of being on their own, of living their own lives, of making their own contacts—of growing independence.

It is true that the friends they select may not always fit in with our standards, or with their own standards, for that matter. They may pick friends, for one thing, to help them live through old feelings that need to be lived through belatedly before they can make more mature choices.

Just as Bruce's mother would have chosen Bruce's friends to help her live through an old sense of inferiority, so our children may choose their friends to help them live through similar feelings.

Little mousy Priscilla, for instance, chooses flashy, forward Enid as her chum. Enid is almost a part of her own self. When they go to parties together, she relies on Enid to engage boys

[182]

in conversation. "I learn from her, I think. She makes me feel stronger."

To Priscilla, Enid's allegiance is all-important. She has in her an ally who is helping her "get her man," just as she wanted to have Mother be an ally to help her stand in right with Father in the earlier days.

Lorna, a large, handsome girl, somewhat too heavy, chose unattractive, sallow Una as her favorite companion. Since Una's father was sick and unemployed, Lorna showered the girl with presents; gave her clothes, books, cookies. Through this friendship Lorna, in her way, was gaining the importance she needed at this time. As she grew older and thinned down and found herself appealing to boys, the intensity of her friendship with Una dissolved.

In one way or another, in their friendships, especially in early and middle adolescence, girls may be working out earlier rivalry feelings toward their mothers that they may still carry unrecognized in their unconscious minds. Similarly, boys may be working out their unconscious feelings toward their fathers.

As parents, we do not need to stop to decipher what each friendship means. The important thing for us to know is that they do have reasons for being. As we understand and accept this fact, we will bear with our children as they live through these friendships. We won't need to bestow the telling look of disapproval that gets our child's back up and makes him cling to a friendship harder and longer than he otherwise might.

We need not pretend or be dishonest about our own feelings. But our focus will not be so all-on-ourselves if we understand that the adolescent's feelings are important for him to live through. His wild enthusiasms need not be taken as enduring. In the early teens, especially, he is likely to vacillate from one type of friend to another.

Sometimes he will come to us, almost pleadingly demanding an opinion of his friends. For the moment he needs it; even though he throws it over the next.

In any event, if we resist him too strongly in his selection of friends, he may, just to resist us, persist harder and longer in making choices we dislike. He will then uphold his friends, do or die, in order to go against us and what we wish.

This is true not only in choices as to friends of the same sex but true as well in choices as to "dates." By the way we handle the matter of dating, we communicate to our young ones whether or not we approve, not only of the girl or boy friend of the moment, but also of their ability to handle the whole boy-girl situation and themselves in it.*

What to do, though, when friends are actually antisocial, "wild" or "destructive"? This is a far more serious state of affairs. Then the parental foot may have to be put down heavily. "No, this is out. We cannot have this." However, even these strong, direct forbiddings may be ineffective if the youngster's drive to work out his problems through such friendships is too compelling. By hook or crook he may find ways of continuing with them, secretively behind parental backs.

Such was the case with Sheila, a little fair-haired girl as innocent-looking a child as one could find. She came from a home where "she had everything," from a swimming pool to the most gorgeous clothes.

"I don't know what went wrong." Her father's knuckles showed white as he told the story.

"I can't imagine either," her mother sobbed as she chewed at her lips.

Sheila and three of her friends had been caught shoplifting. In the knitting bag that Sheila carried demurely, one day's

* See Chapter 10.

[184]

"haul" included a sun suit, a blouse, nylon stockings and three pairs of ear clips.

"But you don't need them, Sheila. Why did you do it?" her mother wailed.

"It's clear enough," asserted her father. "It's all on account of the friends she goes with. She's got to drop them. Then it will stop."

Under duress, Sheila did drop them. But soon she was in with an even wilder gang. There were sex offenses this time instead of stealing.

It was only after long-term psychotherapy that Sheila came out of it, equipped with self-understanding that brought new wisdom and health.

To Sheila, the forbiddings to go with the "gang" had been echoes of other forbiddings. Recently, her parents had disapproved of the one boy with whom she most wanted to date. Before that . . . "so long before" . . . Sheila couldn't remember exactly . . .

From Sheila's mother, however, many of the facts were brought to light. In her anxiety to train her small daughter, she'd striven too hard. The initial forbiddings had come very early. Sheila had not been fed when her small body had craved food; she'd been fed by the clock. Her little hands, seeking pleasure, had been tied to the bedposts. She'd been kept starched and clean and had not been allowed to play in mud or suds. When Sheila, grown a little older, had sought her father's company in tomboyish fashion, she'd been reprimanded. "Be dainty. Be sweet."

In her unconscious mind Sheila had put these things together. She interpreted them to mean that her mother was against her and did not want her to have any "fun." True, she had been given many material possessions. But the primitive, early cravings had gone begging as had also the wish for more understanding and love. And so Sheila had grown, forever wanting more than she had.

The problem in Sheila had been formed one way. The same problem can have quite different beginnings in other girls or boys. Ordinarily behind such behavior the wish-for-more-than-I've-had joins up with the wish-for-asserting-anger against a parent who is seen or imagined as depriving. It's as if a child were saying, "My mother—or my father—doesn't want to let me have what gives me pleasure . . . Okay, then I'll get it however I can . . ."

In some instances, if shackles that are actually too strict or unreasonable are released, a child begins to seek pleasure more rationally. In some instances, if he can get new light on the stirrings of his body for pleasure, this will release his anxiety and make him feel less driven to throw over the shackles of his own conscience. In other instances, as with Sheila, the better part of wisdom is to seek professional help.

Fortunately, in some of the camps set up by probation departments, in some chaplain's offices, in some youth groups and in some schools as well as in guidance clinics and private offices, both individual and group work are being done to help boys and girls whose problems lead them into troublesome paths.

Ordinarily, however, the adolescent's friendships are more positive and serve a more wholesome purpose. He needs us to bear with him in his quick shifts and "undying loyalties." He needs also to have us listen to the gripes he makes about his friends without our inserting gibing comments about his "villain" of today having been his "hero" of yesterday. He needs us to have faith that he will move with the passing of time into more mature choices.

He needs us all along to be sensitive to our own feelings about his friends. If we find critical attitudes entering, we'll do well to ask ourselves as honestly as we can: Are our objections founded on the fact that these friends are actually unde-

sirable or harmful? Or are our objections based on old prejudices and wishes which should not be intruding now into the
lives and choices of our boys and girls?

As long as a relationship seems actually to be heartening
and wholesome, our youngsters need to know that we will go
with them on it, welcoming their friends in easy, uncritical
fashion, as best we can.

TWO WORDS ON CHOOSING CLOTHES

To an adolescent, feelings about clothes are apt to go beyond the old adage that "clothes make the man." Clothes *are*
the man. His clothes, as it were, are a part of him. By them will
he—or she—be judged.

The inordinate concentration on appearance, the fussiness
over a shirt's not being loose enough, jeans not tight enough,
skirts not long enough, ties in with the feeling that the person
and the clothes are one. It's as if our boy or girl were saying,
"If my clothes are all right, then I'm all right; if they're wrong,
then I'm awry."

The strutting or posing or gawking by the hour in front of
the mirror is not so often vanity. It is anxiety. It's as if he were
appraising not only his clothes but himself and his body.

Concern over his body is natural in these years, as we have
seen. Part of it ties in with the growing awareness of sexual
changes and the thrust of sexual feelings. Anything that he
feels is "wrong" with his body or with his sexual feelings is apt
to make him more self-conscious about his clothes.

Even the apparent unconcern of "the-sloppier-the-better"
attitude may in truth be the opposite.

Says Rick's father sternly, "Why on earth, Rick, do you have
to keep looking so sloppy?"

"Why?" Rick returns nonchalantly. "Don't you know, Dad,
that's the style?"

The denial of interest in clothes may be denial of concern
over his body or over himself. He may once more be using the

[187]

hiding technique we've heard about before. Or he may be harking back to earlier, more babyish stages of development where messiness was the prime joy in life.

As we well know by now, one thing that may throw the adolescent back to an earlier stage is the sense of rivalry that so

Daughter: "Just between us, Daddy, don't you think I look much more terrific than mother in this dress of hers?"

often creeps in with growing up—the boy's rivalry with father; the girl's rivalry with mother.

"I wish I were as attractive as my mother," groans Emily. "She's old, it's true, but isn't she stunning? And," with envy apparent, "you should see her pictures when she was young! I could never equal her. Never."

With guilt over her own rivalry feelings Emily feels twinges of insecurity, for one thing, in selecting her clothes. She wants to do her own choosing and yet she wants her mother's approval, which means that in a way she is dependent on her mother's choice.

Similar feelings exist in many a youngster. They swing from wanting to choose independently to wanting help or approval dependently.

"Tell me, Mother, do I look all right? Isn't my skirt too bunchy? Isn't my hair terrible?" pleads Eva. But in the next breath she waves her mother's opinion aside and exclaims with utter disdain, "Moth-er, you're foolish to say this isn't becoming. This, I repeat, is what all the girls wear!"

"Look, Mum," crows Clara, exultantly pirouetting in front of the mirror, "this is just gorgeous! This is really my type of dress!" Then, in sudden pause, with yearning for Mother's praise peeking from behind the wish for self-assertion, "I realize, of course, that it doesn't suit your taste, but honestly don't you think it just suits mine?"

What these attitudes sum up to in our day-to-day living makes the choosing of clothes a subject of tender and often irrational moment.

"Why can't they be content with hand-me-downs?" Or "Why do they want them?" Father's overcoat. Mother's earrings. Like having a claim to a parent's fame. Or like wanting none of it because of the wish and drive for fame of one's own. As for discards from older brother or sister, these are strictly to be hung on the limb of a tree to be carried off by the wind!

Borrowing, however, is another matter. Here one's own choice functions. When one wants, it's fine to borrow another person's attractiveness, as it were. It's intriguing to show how neatly one can outrival the other person by looking better and then, just as neatly, to salve one's conscience and regain one's own individuality by returning the possession. It's like stepping into another person's shoes with freedom to step out at will and get back into one's own with a sigh of comfort.

But when one's own shoes are borrowed, this is another matter. "Mother, please," with indignation, "won't you tell Blanche to stay out of my drawers!"

How to keep peace is a futile question. The wrangling and fussing between brethren—this is a normal and wholesome part of growing up.

[189]

At this age, too, shopping may become a major issue.

Says Steve, "Gee, Ma, I don't know what kind of slacks to get. Won't you or Dad go with me?"

Says Mother, "Steve, you make me weary. Last week you said you wanted to be independent; you'd decide for yourself."

"But, Ma!" with a kind of giving-up shrug, "last week it didn't matter so much. This week . . . well, Betty's going out with me and I have to look right."

No matter the reason, in one mood, at one moment, a youngster feels uncertain. In another mood, at another moment, the independent spirit rules. It's wise when he feels wobbly to come to the rescue, not with the clinging or clenching grasp but with a hand that gives willing support and then willingly lets go and withdraws to leave the youngster free on his own when the sense of being stronger is restored.

Probably the hardest thing for both child and parent to tolerate is an overbearing insistence that the parent knows best.

Scene observed in a store

Onlooker (to herself): "What a nice-looking youngster. About sixteen, I'd judge. Looks the way her mother used to, I'd imagine, before her mother started turning puffy and fat."

Salesgirl: "What can I show you?"

Mother: "My child wants a robe."

The salesgirl disappears behind the scenes and returns presently. Meanwhile the mother has been lecturing her daughter. "Now, remember, we haven't all day. I don't want your usual namby-pambiness and hesitance. It's about time you learned to choose things for yourself. That's why I brought you . . ."

Mother (to salesgirl): "Let me see what you have."

The daughter slips silently into several robes while the mother makes running comments. "No, I don't like that one. The color's unbecoming." . . . "No, that one's impractical. Too fluffy!" . . . "Let me feel that material. No, it wouldn't stand up . . ."

Finally, with the trying on of a loose little number of bright, flowered challis, the girl's face lights up.

Daughter: "Isn't this perfect?"

Mother: "Try that one over there, dear. The old-rose flannel wrapper with the white binding on the lapels."

Daughter: "Please, Mother, not that one. It's so old-fashioned and mannish."

Mother: "It's one of those good sound styles that never goes out of date. As for it's being mannish, I've had one for years. Come now, my dear, try it on."

Sulkily daughter tries it. Stands in front of the long mirror, looking disgusted. Takes it off.

Mother: "Put it back on, dear, I want to have a look at the shoulders . . ."

Daughter obeys. Puts it on, takes it off grimly. Then picks up the flowered challis and slips into it again. Preens in front of the mirror, obviously delighted with herself in it.

Mother: "It's no use considering that one. It's not at all suitable."

Daughter: "But, Mother, why not?"

Mother: "Come, come, my dear. Make up your mind. We haven't all day."

Daughter: "But, Mother, I . . ."

Mother (to the salesgirl): "That's just fine! Send the old-rose one."

Daughter: "But, Mother, I don't like it."

Mother (as if to herself): "Yes, indeed, it's by far the most practical. And the color's good too."

Daughter: "I hate the color."

Mother: "And you need the warmth."

Daughter: "I get too hot as it is with the way you turn the heat up . . ."

Mother (to the salesgirl): "Send it."

Daughter: "I won't wear it."

Mother: "Come along, my dear. I'm in a hurry. You're just plain spoiled."

As the mother stalks off, the girl dragging behind her, the salesgirl turns to the onlooker with a wry smile.

"Can you beat it? Won't mothers ever learn? You can't treat the new generation that way. I wonder, who's spoiled?"

The moral is clear! The conclusion obvious! The same words of wisdom apply to many things. In the matter of home chores or home jobs, in the matter of friends, in the matter of clothes . . .

Give your teen-ager
HIS CHOICE WHEREVER POSSIBLE.
When you choose to choose for him
claim and admit it.
Be honest and firm.

WHEN YOUR CHOICE MUST BE UPHELD

"But," you exclaim. "I am firm. I do insist. I keep on insisting. All in vain. He keeps on going his own way and disregards me."

Again you may need to check yourself. Have you slipped back into your own old way? Have you been disregarding your teen-ager? Have you been neglecting to accept his feelings? In your effort to have him regulate his acts, have you been turning your focus onto his behavior alone?

He likes a certain friend. She likes a certain dress. You have good grounds to disapprove of both. Do you listen nonetheless to know how your children feel about them?

[192]

And when you differ and ask that your adolescent act in accordance, do you expect him to accept this sweetly? Or do you think back on how you used to feel when similar things happened to you in your adolescence? Did you feel sweet?

Remind yourself once again to *expect* your adolescent to rave or gripe when you gainsay him, remembering that there will be more chance of his accepting what you say about *how he should act* when you have accepted what he says about *how he feels*.

12. If Your Child's Adopted

The number of adopted children in this country today is legion. And the problems and wonderings of the many adoptive parents are much alike.

If you are an adoptive parent, you no doubt got your child only after a long period of searching and waiting. You were "inspected" and looked over carefully to see if you could offer a suitable home. Any warm little ideas you might have cherished about its being "noble" to take in a poor little waif had run pattering long since down the street. By the time you found the baby, you felt as if a favor were being bestowed upon you which you somehow didn't quite deserve. The privilege was supposedly all yours; not the baby's. It's probable that you felt lower than a worm and abjectly grateful and glad, and yet a bit resentful, although this may have gone unconfessed even to yourself. For, in taking this step you had, in all probability, gone through many struggles. Had you not, perhaps, struggled long hours to bring around unwilling family members? Had you not, perhaps, braved objections and mustered courage to withstand the disapproval you felt was still there underneath an external layer of smiles? And, most painful of all, had you not needed to quiet your own doubts and wonderings?

You may not have known it, but this last was the hardest and took the greatest amount of courage. For, even though the prospect of having a baby was wonderful, still, if faced with absolute honesty, the fact of adopting one was a kind of acknowledgment of failure on your part.

"We've tried and tried, and although there's no reason, still we don't have a baby . . ." (Note the implication: one has tried and failed.) . . . "We can't have a baby because it would be too risky after the two we lost on account of the Rh factor." (Again the same story of not being able to achieve what one wishes most, a babe of one's own flesh and blood.)

"But," says one adoptive parent after another, "this child that we've taken, he *is* our own. There's no difference."

There need be no difference in the love, the opportunity and the understanding which one gives the baby. But there is often a difference in one's attitude toward oneself. There is often a kind of apology, unconscious though it may be. An apology for not having been capable of achieving the biological goal of living, the reproducing of kin.

It is because of this very apology that many an adoptive parent approaches his child with hesitance and an anxiety which he tries hard to deny.

Then, as his child grows, he find that certain moments prove more difficult than others. In general these are moments which hark back to that devastating small or large sense of failure that went lurking about in the beginning, either out in the open or stealthily under cover.

It is of these more crucial moments that we shall talk. For even though some of them are past long before the teen age, still, to remedy any consequent errors, we must reach from the vantage point of our children's adolescence back into awareness of what has happened before.

FIRST CRUCIAL MOMENT: AM I ADOPTED?

A great many parents have met this question with directness and honesty. In the beginning, even before the child himself wondered or asked, they told him about searching for a baby whom they could love and care for since no baby had been born to them.

Many parents have told in story form about choosing the adopted child. Possibly while their child was still in the pre-school years, they discovered a book that could be read or followed in telling the story of looking for and finding the baby for whom they yearned.

Possibly they relied on their own ingenuity to tell their own story.

"Tell me the story about how you got me," Louise, who is six, asks her father for the fiftieth time.

"We-ell," he begins, "as I've told you before, your mommie and I wanted a baby and we waited and waited but no baby came . . ."

"And"—Louise picked up the tale by now fondly familiar—"you sat at the breakfast table very sad and said you wished there was a baby in your house."

"And . . ."

"You sat at the dinner table very sad and wished it some more . . ."

"And . . ."

"Near lunch time when you were at your business and Mommie was shopping or sewing or filling the car with gas, you both kept wishing and wishing . . ."

"That's right."

"And then?"

"One day a telegram came and it said there was a fine baby for us. We should come right away."

"So you packed up your big suitcase for you. And Mommie packed up her middle-sized suitcase for her. And you and Mommie both packed up the tiny, baby suitcase for me with diapers and everything in it and you took a great big basket with lots of bottles and you got on the train and you went to where I was. And you saw me . . ."

"And we said, 'That's the most lovable baby we ever met . . .' "

"And that was ME . . ."

Then followed the tale of the return journey. The joy of the parents and the chuckling funny worrisomeness of their wonderings if they, who had never before had a baby, would know what to do if she cried . . .

"You would look for a pin and an air bubble 'cause you didn't know if it was the pin scream or the air-bubble cry and you thought you'd ask the conductor on the train if he had any babies and if he knew. Only then you found out for yourself it wasn't the pin and it wasn't the air bubble, it was just me saying in cry language that I wanted a hug . . ."

Some parents have told the story of adoption early; others have delayed. Some are uncertain whether or not their adolescent children know. "We're so worried," Kent's mother confided. "We've never told him. We felt he should believe he was born to us. But the other day I ran into one of our former neighbors from the district where we used to live. They moved over this way about a year ago and she told me Kent and her boy are in some of the same classes in junior high school. Then she asked me if we'd ever told Kent about being adopted, and she said it was terrible not to. If he found out from other people it might be a dreadful shock.

"So here we are. It's dawned on us at last that we've made an awful mistake not to tell him. Suppose he finds out! Or worse! Suppose he's found out already?"

After much more discussion of their own attitudes, these parents decided that making a clean breast of the matter would clear the atmosphere.

"We've got to admit this mistake just as all parents need to

[197]

admit mistakes of one sort or another. For what parents haven't made mistakes of some sort by the time their children are in their teens?

"Kent may be mad at first, just as any child is mad when he discovers that he has been excluded from confidences which might have made him feel closer and might have given him a greater sense of belonging. But we'll try to remember that getting this anger out is healthier than keeping it in.

"We'll try to remember that Kent's relationship with us will rest on a more solid foundation if we tell him the truth and then let him be real in his anger and accept it for what it is. We'll try to remember that after his anger has drained sufficiently, his confidence in us will have a better chance to grow." And so they followed out their plan by talking with Kent one evening.

"We've made a great mistake . . . This we realize now. And, believe us, we're sorry. We did it because we thought it best. We wanted to protect you. But we've learned that such protection separates parents and child. Perhaps you've even felt we were hiding something from you?"

"No," said Kent. "No." And then, "Yes," quite suddenly. And for all of his thirteen years he burst into tears. "You mean I'm not really your child?"

"But you are our child, Kent!"

"But," with a great sob, "I wasn't born from you!"

There followed anger and blame and more tears. But they weathered it, with father and mother pulling together. And in the end, the light came into Kent's eyes and the dawning of truth.

"You mean my bearing mother left me right after I was born?"

"Yes."

"What kind of a mother do you call that?" with sudden

contempt. "A fish mother, I call it! That's what fish parents do. They lay their eggs and swim off . . . That may be love to a fish but it's not to a person. *You're* my real parents; not those fish!"

SECOND CRUCIAL MOMENT: WHO GAVE ME BIRTH?

Sooner or later the adopted child comes upon the question of biological beginnings. Sooner or later he recognizes, as Kent did, that he was not "born from you."

Always this is a hard moment. For it harks back to the sense of failure we had in the beginning in regard to our own biological competence.

There are two approaches to this question. One approach is made in the belief that a child needs to feel that the biological parents first and foremost wanted him. However, they were either unable to keep him, or thoughtfully and wisely sought better care for him than they themselves could provide. The thought here is that the biological parents should be represented as responsible people who took responsibility for the best good of their child.

The other approach is that the biological parents need no defending. Quite honestly, they were not good parents to this particular child, no matter what the circumstances were. Why, then, build up a good parent picture to which this child, now, may attach wishful fantasies?

Invariably in adolescence there are times when all children, whether adopted or not, feel that their parents do not understand them, that they are out of contact, that they are "bad" parents as it were.

Says Harold, who is not adopted, "I used to think I must have belonged originally to parents who would have understood me better. Only they got me mixed up some way in the hospital and these parents got me instead."

Harold, however, essentially knows that this is fantasy. "I'd often like parents who did understand me better. But you have to learn to make allowances."

On the other hand, Effy, who is adopted, attaches more weight to the fantasy. "It isn't just an idea. I'm sure of it. If my original parents had only kept me I'd have been much happier than with these parents. My parents were good people. My adopting parents told me. They were so tremendously interested in my welfare that they were willing to make the supreme sacrifice of giving me to a family they thought could provide more . . . But I ask you, provide more of what? Clothes and things. Why, I'd rather go hungry if I could only live with people who thought so much of me they even sacrificed themselves . . ."

To Effy, the fantasy of "good parents" is firmly fastened to the biological unknowns, boosted by praise they have had from her adoptive parents. Onto the adoptive parents' heads she has just as firmly pasted the picture of all that is "bad."

It is natural for any parent to be labeled in a child's mind as "good" at some moments, as "bad" at other moments. But sometimes adoptive parents in their zeal over a "fair deal" to the biological parents give their child a fantasied "all-good" picture of the biological parents, leaving themselves more open to the "bad-parent" role.

For this reason and also because it fits in with what some parents believe more honest, instead of painting the biological parents' picture in glowing colors, they put the thing differently.

"Some mothers want a baby," says Lester's mother to seven-year-old Lester. "Only they can't have one. For reasons we don't quite understand, no baby starts to grow in these particular mothers' bodies. Other mothers don't want a baby and yet a baby does grow inside. And so there's this thing called 'adoption.' The mother who doesn't want the baby gives it up and the parents who do want the baby are glad as glad can be to get it."

"Yes," says Lester, "that's what you and Daddy did with me. You're my caring-for-me daddy and mommy; not my seed daddy and mommy."

"And it's the caring for that counts."

As for being wanted, these parents feel, it doesn't matter whether the biological parents did or did not want this child.

"What difference does it make if they wanted or didn't want you? We wanted you so much ourselves. And," in echo of Lester's statement, "it's the caring for that counts."

In your own particular instance, you may have followed the policy of defending the biological parents and you may still feel that you did this believing honestly in it. On the other hand, if you feel you've made a mistake and are angry at yourself for it, again it isn't too late.

You don't even have to make very serious business out of it. As long as you are straight inside yourself about not needing to preserve an artificially beautiful image, you can say sincerely although casually, "Sometimes I know you feel misunderstood. All children do. You probably think if we were your blood parents instead of your adoptive parents, we'd understand you better. We've painted such a glowing picture of them we've given ourselves an unfair deal. But no matter whom you'd have been with, you'd have had 'bad' moments all the same. Like now. At least we know now that sometimes you hate us roundly and feel we're terrible."

"You said it," John growled. "You expressed it exactly. Only," with a broad grin suddenly emerging, "only those other parents, they might have been worse."

THIRD CRUCIAL MOMENT: WERE THEY MARRIED?

Usually during adolescence, the adopted child wonders whether his biological parents were married or whether he was born out of wedlock. Understandably, he is concerned.

"I didn't know what on earth to tell Pam," one mother confessed.

"Why didn't you tell her the truth?"

"I thought that she'd feel some social stigma." As if Pam as a baby had been responsible to society for having been born!

"She might feel somehow less good!" As if a baby were more good or less good in view of whether or not his parents have had a marriage license! . . .

Obviously it's absurd! And yet an enormous amount of social stigma has been attached to illegitimate births. However, this attitude is on the wane. We are realizing more and more that granted an ordinary, healthy heredity, the emotional climate in which a child is nurtured has the power to help him grow straight and strong.

A baby's parents' sex relations may be legal or otherwise. But the baby is the same baby, conceived by the same act and brought into the world by the same process. He is quite unaware of and not at all responsible for his parents' having or not having a marriage license. He's the same baby endowed with the same spirit and health and energy whether he is born in wedlock or not.

Far more important is our own attitude. Are we as adoptive parents fearful because this child's biological parents were not married that he or she may follow in the same path? Are we afraid because of this false bugaboo to tell our child the truth?

As with other things, honesty is the best policy. It's the way it's presented that counts. It's our own feeling about it that communicates itself.

And so, when the adopted child asks—as he may ask ordinarily when he reaches adolescence—if you feel bothered, talk it over with each other, with yourself, with a counselor.

The fact of illegitimacy need carry no stigma to you, no barrier, no cause for condemnation, no reason for shame.

FOURTH CRUCIAL MOMENT: WHENEVER ANGERS ARISE

It is often hard for an adoptive parent to stand the angry moments that arise in every child. It is as if shades of the old, initial fear of failure were rising in an ominous whisper: "If my child shows me he doesn't love me, it proves that my apprehensions then were right." Frequently another thought follows, very unfortunately: "I've got to be a perfect parent in order to prove I'm not a failure."

"I can't discipline Allen," says Allen's mother. "He's simply obnoxious. And yet I just can't put my foot down as firmly as I know I ought."

She explored the problem further and she found she was afraid that if she made Allen unhappy, even with the temporary unhappiness which all children have in moments when they must be gainsaid, he might wish he'd landed in some other home.

"I mayn't be cross. I mayn't be nasty. I must never let myself admit that sometimes I wish to goodness I hadn't gotten this child," in the very same way that every biological parent wishes at times that he hadn't begotten his.

It's natural for every biological parent to wish this in the difficult spaces. It's natural for the adoptive parent too! It's natural for any parent to admit it if he is honest and unafraid of how he feels.

Children have problems. Children are nuisances. Children have their times of failure. Children at moments are less than their parents would wish. And in adolescence, children's ideas and ideals depart from the ideas and ideals that their parents have lived by.

Such things are natural. They have nothing to do with whether a child is adopted or not.

And so, if you are an adoptive parent, let one precept guide you:

> Be natural
> Be honest
> Be real—
> Nice or nasty—
> Those are the things that really count.

13. If You've Been Separated or Divorced

"When there's trouble at home you feel very bad," writes a fourteen-year-old. "Sometimes it starts over the mirror or bobby pins or anything you want first but have to wait for." These are little troubles. But there are bigger ones too.

"Some people have very big arguments over big things, like separations or things to do with court. If they have families they sow a little seed called grief and with their quarreling they help it grow and the family is a family no more but a bunch of people that hate each other." Children sense and are upset by the emotional divorce which always precedes the actual separation. The legal divorce comes as a culmination. Meanwhile the little seed called grief has inevitably grown very big. However, if the situation is properly handled, the child's grief can be decreased.

If the trouble started much earlier when your child was small, he may have wondered secretly about it and imagined many things in his childish mind. Very likely he denied vigorously, and still does, that he was worried. But underneath he was bothered nonetheless.

If the separation happened later in his childhood, the act of his parents' separating may have thrown him back into wonderings belonging to an earlier time in his development.

It is almost always hard for children to understand why their parents must separate. What they don't know of fact, they supply with fiction. And their fiction usually springs from things fantasied far in the past.

EVERY CHILD WONDERS: WHAT WAS WRONG?

When a child feels that he does not know what has actually happened to break up his parents' marriage, he is apt to be more disturbed than he would be if he were taken into their confidence. He feels isolated and fills the gaps with what he imagines. And many times what he imagines has to do with himself.

Sally, fifteen, a swift whirlwind of a girl, full of energy and leadership suddenly did a rightabout-face. "All the sparkle went out of her," her sensitive home-room teacher explained. "She resigned the vice-presidency of her class and she's moody and morose. Doesn't get her work in. Won't participate. Something's gone wrong . . ."

Something had.

"My father left my mother last week!"

Sally brushed a hurried hand across her eyes and flung back her hair. "I hate to say it but I know it was my fault. I've known from 'way, 'way back it would happen sooner or later. And it did."

A few days before her father's departure there had been a big scene. "My mother'd been out shopping and she got home just as my father got home from work and the first thing they both asked me was, had I practiced. I said 'Yes.' Only that brat of a brother of mine told them I hadn't.

"That was the beginning of the end. My father called me a 'liar' and my mother called me a 'fabricator,' which was at least a little more civilized. Only then my father got mad and said she should say what she meant and call a spade a spade and not a spaddle. And then he turned on me and he said what he's said so often, that I'd be the death of him and I'd be the cause of him and mother divorcing . . . And now I am.

"I've tried to blame my brother. If he hadn't snitched, things wouldn't have exploded. But if I stop being a liar to myself, I know it's me . . ."

As Sally went on talking, her thinking hitched up with thoughts she'd had much further back. "Now they're separated I'd like to go live with my father. If I weren't scared my mother would just about kill me, I'd say so. I've always wanted to. Like when I was a little girl I'd make up stories. See, I brought a picture book I drew when I was small."

Sally paged the leaves and pointed. "This picture's when I was about six. I'm cooking dinner and Daddy's bringing me a bunch of flowers and my mother and brother aren't there . . . And here in this picture Daddy and I are going to the store to buy ice cream . . . and here in this one Daddy's taking me to the beach! I pretended that Mother'd moved away. I'm not sure, but I think I made up that she'd be gone for always. Only I knew I was bad to dream up that one. So I told myself it was for the summer in summerime and for Christmas at Christmastime and for Easter in the spring. What it came to as a result was practically all year 'round.

"And now Daddy's left me!"

Her imagination took over. "Do you suppose mother found my picture book and showed it to him? And that made them both angry? And that's why he left?"

In Sally's search for an explanation of her father's leaving she had dipped into the past. Dreams of wanting to separate her mother and father were trickling up from the love-rivalry period to join with her present-tense thoughts. She didn't know it was quite natural and normal for every small girl to wish that Mother were out of the picture so that she might have Father all to herself. And so the earlier wishes

[207]

which had made her feel "bad" then were making her feel "bad" now. In consequence, she was all ready and set to believe what her father had flung out repeatedly in his own confusion and anger, "You'll be the cause of our divorce."

Sally was like many other children. When left to their own devices to explain to themselves what has happened, they grow confused. Even very young children then muster fantasies to explain what they otherwise cannot fathom.

Small Howard, four, sits like a wise old man and wheezes. "He's never naughty," his mother comments. "But his asthma started soon after his father left—he was two then."

In his play with a doll family representing Mother and himself, with Father added in order to take him back to the days before his wheezing started, he tells his story. He plays out his scenes with surprising alertness.

The father doll gets mad and scolds the mother. "I don't want eggs for dinner"—he enacts the father's role. "Give me meat," says the father angrily. "Give me meat. Give me meat. Give me meat!"

"No," says the mammy. And she kicks the daddy. She kicks the daddy right out of the door.

In his play, however, he could not let the boy get angry. The very idea made the worry lines and the anxious look reappear.

And then, out came the source of his fear.

"If you get mad you get kicked out. That's what mammies do."

It had happened to Daddy when Daddy got mad. So if *he* got mad it might happen to him.

In similar manner, small Rory showed that he was anxious that his mother would not want him because of another kind of "badness" that he carried on by touching himself after he was in bed at night. His mother might send him away for being "bad" in this fashion just as his mother had sent his father away for whatever kind of "badness" he had carried on.

Child after child shows similar feelings when the parents separate. Something is wrong, very wrong. Was something wrong with Daddy? With Mother? Is something wrong with me? Why did Daddy, or Mother, go away and leave me? Didn't they love me anymore? Did it happen because I was "bad"? . . . This is the worst fear of all.

One thing that can help prevent such fear from piling up is to tell our children about the divorce or separation as simply and clearly as we possibly can. Even if it happened much earlier and you failed to tell him, you can let him in on it now.

GIVE HIM THE FACTS

Don't pretend. Don't make up pretty reasons. No matter how "ugly" the reasons are, they're better straight out to our children, or at least as straight as we can put them.

It's not always easy, however, to get the facts straight.

We ourselves may feel confused about them. Uncertain about what really went wrong. So unclear in our own thinking that it's impossible to clarify the matter to anyone else.

Quite apparently, then, the first step is to put the facts as straight as we can to ourselves.

If you feel confused, try, if you can, to talk the whole thing over with someone. A professional person is best. In any case, talk it over with yourself. Out loud is better than in silent thinking. Even though you may sound silly to yourself at first, as you struggle to put your feelings and thoughts into words they sometimes come clearer. It will then be simpler and easier to share the facts with your child.

"Gina, I'm sure you must have wondered why your father and I separated. I know now I should have told you more about it. But I didn't know this until recently. I thought in an old-fashioned way that I was 'saving you' by keeping quiet. I guess that was silly . . .''

"Yes, Mother, it was," Gina pitched in forthrightly. "Because I've wondered and worried a lot."

When you start you won't need to be long-winded. A simple statement will put the matter out in the open as a first step in the right direction. The important thing is to help your boy or girl feel free to talk about his own feelings and to ask you questions that will lighten his wonderings and doubts as time moves on.

Quite honestly, "Your father loved somebody else better than he loved me," if there was another-woman reason. Or "He went around looking for someone else to love," if it was another-woman-plural deal. Or "We spent so much time quarreling that staying together just wasn't worth it. We figured we'd be more content apart." Or "Being in bed together and loving each other the way married people should in order to feel close and in harmony didn't work out well for us."

Whatever the problem was, or however you see it, be as open and honest about it as you can be.

TELL HIM ABOUT YOUR FEELINGS

If possible, and if you can feel it honestly, try to help your child feel that the other parent is a "good" person but just was not good for you.

If, however, you do not believe this, don't put on an act. Upholding an ideal that to you is anything but an ideal is purposeless. It can do more harm than good in that your child may sense your falseness and come to distrust you, and so lose the security he needs to have you give him.

Margaret's father had left when Margaret was five. His story was a sordid one of staying away night after night; of lurching home drunk in the early mornings. Of nonsupport. And of the final, terrible moment when, after a week of waiting, Margaret's mother had discovered that the little money she had saved and the little jewelry she had inherited had disappeared with her husband.

From that night forward she had neither seen nor heard from him. Not a cent had he contributed to either his wife's or his child's livelihood.

And yet Margaret's mother proclaimed proudly, "I've never said a mean word to Margaret against her father. I've wanted to help her preserve her ideal."

She had felt exceedingly noble. She did not realize that she had actually been living a lie to her daughter.

Meanwhile Margaret had grown into her teens.

"She's a fright," her mother wept. "She's so sulky and selfish. She wants more and more. A new slip. A new dress. Permanents. And now a fur coat I can't possibly get. I try and I try to see that she has what she craves. But it's never enough."

No matter what her mother gave her, Margaret wanted still more.

Came a day, however, when Margaret and her mother both began to see more clearly how things had been. Not knowing the facts, Margaret had tried to put two and two together with her mind's imaginings. Secretly she had loved her father. Secretly she had fantasied that he had loved her better than he had loved her mother. Mother, in consequence, had been angry and had pushed him out. In short, Mother had robbed her of what she had wanted most in life. So Margaret was after something else—anything, everything—to make up for what she thought her mother had taken away.

No wonder nothing was ever enough. Nor could it be, as long as Margaret held onto wanting the impossible: an imaginary hero of a father who had never really existed except in her little-girl mind, where his image still rode in glory.

Had her mother shared the truth with her daughter she would at least not have strengthened this fabulous lie. She

[211]

could never give Margaret her father, but she could give Margaret herself in good faith and with honesty.

This she now belatedly did, and after a time of trial and tribulation, matters improved.

Even if Margaret's father had been a "good" person and just not good for her mother, the false front of loving forgiveness would not have furthered Margaret's security. It never does for any child. Security is furthered far more soundly with the solid truth of a parent's feelings out in the open and shared.

Sharing feelings, however, with one's child is different from burdening him with them. The difference lies in the parent's attitude and in what the parent, himself, is seeking when he tells how he feels.

Telling a child because one wants to relieve him of worry—that is one thing. Telling him because one wants to relieve oneself—this is something else.

Richard's mother did the last.

Says fourteen-year-old Richard, "Since my father left, I'm supposed to be everything to my mother. She has no one else, she says, with whom to share her problems. So she expects me to be the man of the house."

Side by side with this, a memory kept creeping up into Richard's mind which he colored with unrealistic fears. He'd heard his father say to his mother many times earlier, "I'll kill any man you dare take up with." And now his mother expected him to be a man—her man—the man whom his imagination prompted him to identify as the one his father would kill.

"I'm in a spot," he confessed in desperation. "I'm a mess-up. I can't keep my mind on my studies. I can't do a thing."

Richard's mother's kind of sharing was for the purpose of using his shoulders to weep on. They weren't broad enough.

No child's are. She would have done better if she had used her pillow at night. She would have done best, though, had she been able to share her feelings with him prompted by a sincere wish to help her son rather than to make a husband out of him.

Lon's father did better in the talks they had while Lon was spending the summer with him.

"I used to tell you, Lon," he began, "that I thought your mother was wonderful. I'll bet though you knew I didn't."

"You hit it, Pop. I knew you didn't and I knew you weren't fooling anyone. But what did make me worry was that you were trying to sell me a bill of goods. It made me wonder about me and you . . ."

"What do you mean, Lon?"

"Well, Pop, you see it's this way. You'd say Mother was swell. And you didn't mean it. So when you'd tell me I was swell, I thought maybe that was some kind of boloney too."

"I can't blame you."

"It kept me from having enough confidence in you to ask the questions I wanted to. So I've kept on worrying about what really happened between you and Mother."

"It's hard to tell, Lon. Not because I don't want to tell you. I've learned that it's right that I should and I do want to. But what happened between your mother and me was so intangible. Nothing definite. She picked on me and I picked on her. She criticized continuously and I couldn't take it. She was never satisfied for some reason. Part of it probably was me. That may sound noble but I think it's the truth. But part of it was her. It probably went back into her own childhood to things that happened then that made her want more from a husband than a husband could give. At least this husband. I know now that my sensitivity to her criticism went back into my childhood too.

[213]

"No matter what it was, I hated her—yes, hated her, literally, for her shrewishness to me and her lack of loving and her demands . . ."

Lon nodded in sixteen-year-old, mature understanding. "She treated you one way. She treated me another. So you developed one set of feelings toward her and I developed another. And each of us has a right to our own stand. That's what liberty in a democracy means."

LET HIM TELL YOU ABOUT HIS FEELINGS TOO

When marriage ends in separation or divorce, a person is bound to be bitter. You are probably no exception. As long as you can make it clear sincerely that you feel bitter because your former husband or wife made *you* unhappy, and that your resentment is connected with what went on between the two of you, your youngster can be more free to feel his own way. As you let him have his own voice, he can be well disposed or not according to his own choice and dictates.

Most probably your child will have piled up anger at both of you for separating. This anger he needs to bring out directly, not in acts that hide the intent but in words that make it clear.

Take Amy, who was thirteen, as a case in point.

Amy stopped eating after her father left. On the advice of her doctor, Amy's mother sought psychological help. Among other things she learned that lack of appetite, lying, stealing, listlessness, poor concentration and a dozen and one other problems can be expressions of anger as surely as a raging temper.

Among other things, Amy was angry because of the divorce. Unconsciously she was showing her anger through her behavior. "So the next time she sits and stares at her food and tells you she doesn't like what you give her, try putting the anger into more direct words for her. Show her also that you still love her and that you understand it's natural for her to feel as she does. Then maybe she'll pick up enough courage to tell you more about it herself. Don't push. Don't prod. Just open the subject. When she knows that you accept the fact that she may be angry, it will probably come eventually of its own accord."

Next evening at the dinner table, Mother looked at Amy's mad, stubborn face and she said, "You look so furious. And I know you must be. I would be too if I were in your place. It's not a happy thing to have a mother who can't give you what you want most in life—your dad. So, of course you're mad . . ."

"I'm not," from Amy huffily.

Her mother said nothing more at the moment. But a short while later, when she went past Amy's chair to take her own empty plate out, she put a comforting hand on her daughter's shoulder. For just a moment. And then, as she went on she turned and gave her daughter a smile that seemed to say "I understand your anger and I still think you're a wonderful girl."

Amy swallowed and gulped and a little smile stole over her face in return. She didn't say anything. But she began to eat.

Three days passed. And all unexpectedly there came a torrent of anger and tears. "I don't see, Mother, why you had to do it. You're supposed to be grown up, you two. And yet you acted worse than children. You don't think I knew how you fought. You thought it was hidden. But your tight faces spoke up louder than words . . ."

And then, somewhat shamefaced, "I guess I was figuring how to get even. I said to myself, 'I'll starve. And then they'll be sorry.' But now I feel better. I don't have to go 'round the barn. I can tell you straight that I'm mad."

From out of a sea of faces, a man rises in the audience, waves his hand and asks, "When you've been divorced and one of you remarries, whose children are whose?"

To him, to the audience and to the speaker, his question was confusing. To his children doubtless too. So much depends on the individual circumstances with their individual variations that generalizing about the situation becomes very difficult.

Here, for instance, is a father who has had his children with him all along. The separation occurred when the boy was four and the girl two. At that time the mother had been ill and unable to care for the children. A year later the father remarried. The new mother was warm and wholesome in her relationship with the little ones. Five years passed. Then the mother, finally recovered, remarried and wondered whether she should take her children back.

Fortunately the situation was discussed amicably and with the best interests of the children in mind. They had built security in the home with their father and stepmother. So, even though it was a blow to their actual mother, she decided with wisdom and generosity not to break into the stable strand of their lives except as a good friend with whom they would visit from time to time. She let the stepmother remain "Mother" essentially in their minds.

Here, similarly, is a mother who in more typical fashion has kept her child with her. She has remarried and so has the father. Again the stability of one home is decided on. The new father adopts the child, much to the child's joy and relief. "Now I can put my initials on my lunch box and they'll be the same as my mom has on her watch."

In another home, however, the name situation has not been so happily solved. Shirley's father insists he will not "give up" his daughter. So Shirley, fifteen, accosts him in straightforward indignation.

"Let's face it," she exclaims. "Maybe, as you say, I am disloyal to you, but I can only tell you how I feel. Mel's been my father now for almost ten years. You have your way of life. He has his and I've got used to his more than to yours. I want to stay friends with you, but I'm telling you right now if you keep on objecting to my using Mel's name, I won't be your friend. I'll be your daughter in name only. And I certainly can't see the use of that."

On the other hand, Blythe, sixteen, counts on being identified with his father. "As long as I can't stay with him, I can at least have his name stay with me."

Whatever the motives, if it is practical to do so, the child's choice of name should be taken into account. If a change is not practical in terms of the adults' wishes or in terms of other material considerations, at least listening to and accepting the youngsters' feelings can sometimes ease the pressure for him.

When there are stepsisters or -brothers, the name situation as well as other considerations may become more acute.

"Do you love me as well as you love your own flesh-and-blood boy?" asks Donny, thirteen, referring to the sixteen-year-old whom his stepmother had brought from a former marriage.

Later, Donny's attractive, still-young stepmother said that her first inclination was to say to Donny, "Don't talk like that." But she stopped herself, luckily, before she started and turning to him thoughtfully answered, "Yes, I can see how you'd feel, Donny. Tell me more about it."

"He was mad, do you know?" she recounted later. "Mad as a hornet that his father hadn't found me before he was born. I told him I was mad too. I'd have gained a lot if I'd been able to have both Donny and his father sooner. On the other hand, being older and more mature myself when I'd found them, I was able to love them both even more."

It was then Donny's turn to look thoughtful. "I see," he said pensively. "There *can* be advantages in being the child a woman gets after she's old."

Jealousies between stepbrothers and stepsisters are natural. So are jealousies among full brothers and sisters. Bringing the gripes and complaints out into the open remains the best policy to pursue.

If the "other" parent remarries and the one with whom the child stays does not remarry, again complications may arise. These usually have to do with one's own jealousy.

"It's hard," confesses one woman, "not to be mad at Vera when she comes home raving over Nate's new wife. I feel she's taking my place and I'm *out*."

Actually this was far from the truth. Vera admired and mimicked her father's new wife just as many girls admire and imitate a beloved teacher. Outside heroes and heroines, as we know, are important assets in adolescence. They help a child move toward emancipation and independence.

Confidently taking one's place as an "outside" hero or heroine can often be of more real value than keeping oneself in the role of a petulant parent forever trying to gain the inside track.

THE PROBLEM OF SEEING AND BEING
WITH THE "OTHER" PARENT

Unless very unusual circumstances exist, a child needs two parents and so he needs to see and be with the parent who has left.

When he is little, he needs also very much to have just one home. For younger children visits are best confined to very short periods of time. As they grow older arrangements may well include longer periods. Summer vacations. Christmas holidays. Perhaps even a complete reversal of what the arrangements have been, as with Humphry, for instance. Humphry

[218]

had chosen a prep school near his father's home. Consequently arrangements were made for his father to take him during the school year and for his mother to have him during vacations, the opposite of the arrangement that had previously prevailed.

What is best for the child is, however, too often lost in the shuffle of the parents' animosity toward each other. It's as if each were using his time with the child to triumph over the other.

"I get furious," exclaimed Vic's mother. "He came home the other day after a week with his father and announced, 'F is for Father and Fun. M is for Mother and Must's.'"

It is natural, of course, that the parent who is visited for brief periods of time should frequently be identified as the "fun" person. The short time together is freer of the hard and arduous routine of living day in and day out with the edges of one personality rubbing against the other's.

It doesn't always work this way, though. Sometimes it boomerangs. The child may turn against the outside parent —for one reason when this parent's strategy is too intense.

"I get uncomfortable with my dad," says Maury. "He tries so hard to get me on his side, and I don't want to take sides. I'm an isolationist, believe me, I am."

Sometimes, too, the parents' jockeying for preferred position is used by the child.

Ruby does this with demonlike cunning.

"My mother," says Ruby to her father with a confiding, innocent air, "she has a new boy friend. I'm not sure whether she'll marry this one or not. But she spends a lot more time in the beauty parlor trying to get the wrinkles out of her neck. And the other morning she didn't get in till five . . ."

Similarly, Ruby reports to her mother, "That father of mine, I think he's the limit. You should see all the things he buys his new wife. He never treated us like that."

In watching the anger arise in each parent, Ruby gloated.

[219]

Unconsciously she has got her father and her mother each in turn to express for her the hostility she herself has been ashamed to avow.

When such matters can be equitably discussed, so much the better. A lot can be gained. Many times, however, the discussion reduces itself to one parent's trying to tell the other how to act.

Dictating this or that behavior one to another is rarely profitable. In the last analysis each one of us can work best on our own part of the picture. On our own relationship to our children. On our own feelings and on our own life.

Perhaps we are trying in too grim a fashion and far too seriously to serve as both parents. This is impossible. It's better to relax at times and not to forget that having fun together is important too.

So is having fun apart.

Finding a balance in one's own life. Getting into busy endeavors. Creative activities. Compatible acquaintanceships. And close friendships, especially if one doesn't remarry. These may help to fills one's days so that a parent does not need to lean too heavily on his child.

14. Let's Not Leave "Emotional Education" Out of Our Schools

Teachers, next to parents, live with teen-agers more than do any other adults. Teachers along with parents bring to bear day-to-day influence. They have a great and grave and important part to play in the adolescent's development.

Because of this, teachers, just like parents, must take the emotional side of the young person's life into consideration with consistent awareness. Neither can leave it to be handled haphazardly as chance dictates.

Insight into how home and family influence the adolescent and how the roots of adolescent personality reach back into infancy and childhood—this should be part of every teacher's equipment. Knowledge of how the school can help the adolescent in his emotional development should similarly become every parent's concern.

For many long years our schools focused on "educating the mind." Their program had to do solely with intellectual education. As time passed, the child's body was brought into focus and a program of physical education was added. Now, at long last, we are recognizing that both intellectual and physical development are tremendously influenced by the emotions. The body can become ill and depleted and can fail to function properly because of emotional undercurrents. So can the mind. Difficulties in concentration, in absorption, in reasoning can occur, as we know, as a result of emotional tensions, even to the extent that failure in school results.

Conversely, when emotions are accorded recognition and are taken into account, not only can failures be prevented but fair performance can be made good and good performance can be made better.

But this is not all.

Our world today is full of troubled children. A few have grown into Hitlers. Multitudes have grown into unhappy persons willing to follow any Hitler in the hope of a life that will be more complete.

Machines have been tended while men have gone wanting.

What a handful of psychiatrists, psychologists and other trained persons can do in terms of *cure* is infinitesimal. What a widespread program of "emotional education" might do in terms of *prevention* is boundless.

If this problem is left in the hands of uninterested politicians, the schools won't do it. But if parents and school people could join hands more firmly in knowing about and insisting on a program of real emotional education, then home and school together might become one of the world's greatest forces. More powerful than armies. For together they would help the young people who *are* the world's future, put warring and warfare into proper proportion and turn their energies more fruitfully into the creation of peace.

DOES YOUR SCHOOL PROVIDE CHANCES FOR
PEER GROUP SUPPORT?

Let us then look briefly at only a few of the things that schools are doing spottily here and there and might be doing more widely if we gave them adequate backing.

Let us look first at the school as a social unit, like a small town.

Ideally this is a town that should be serving as a testing ground in social living. It should be giving opportunities aplenty for trying oneself out, for finding one's place in a city of peers.

It should offer ample and multiple chances for working side by side, for playing together, for enjoying communication and contact. Above all, it should offer opportunity for group support.

This last is imperative for several reasons.

As we know, one of the basic wants of human beings is to feel a sense of belonging.

In the adolescent, however, this sense has often grown somewhat shaky. If he is to mature, he must move out from the belonging that small children have in the family circle. Eventually, if all goes well, he will find another close family unit to give him this needed and nourishing sense. Right now, though, he feels that he has thrust one foot over the threshold of his home but has not yet found a firm spot outside onto which he can set it. He feels somewhat unsteadily balanced on shifting ground. Groups of his own age can and should give him the support he needs during the stretch of these in-between years.

He wants to be liked. Because of his inner revolt from his family and because of his sexual stirrings, he imagines often that they do not like him. Having a group to make him feel liked helps him to like himself better while he weathers the inner doubts and wonderings that go along with growing up.

He no longer wants to live by the prohibitions he learned as a small child. Nor should he. If he does he will never mature.

A child of four may not touch the ornaments on the table

[223]

in the living room. His conscience, such as it is, tells him he must obey this rule of conduct even though his parents are not around. But if at fourteen he is still so concerned with these old rules that he must still obey them, his life obviously will remain too restricted. And yet there are many adolescents whose conscience still dictates the old rules they learned long ago.

New codes and more appropriate restrictions must be acquired. A new conscience, more appropriate to a grown-up body, must grow and develop.

To cite just one more example: The childhood conscience said, "Don't approach any person sexually!" The adult conscience must take exception to this or marriage cannot result.

The teen-ager's peer group can help him acquire the new standards of conduct and control that he seeks and must have. It can bring him the safeguards and prohibitions, the rules and regulations that the youngster, in his own littleness, pushed by the bigness of his newly heightened adolescent impulses, craves and must have.

When he doesn't find a "good" group, he is apt to scout around and get himself into a "bad" one. For even in a "bad" group he may get what he is after: not only companionship to bolster his limited strength but also rules of conduct. In one gang, for example, there are very rigid rules which demand that every boy must remain unbathed for ten days at a time, that he must cohabit with at least one new girl every week, that he must make a certain razor mark on his chest. Absurd or immoral as they are, these rules give him a sense of adherence to codes of conduct which help him to feel more alike and liked. Therefore, if no other peer groups welcome him, he may rush into a gang that gives him such hurtful rather than helpful support. Or he may join a cliquish secret society that puts on false airs and makes him feel big by virtue of snobbishly making others feel small.

[224]

In the junior high or high school typical of our metropolitan areas, the student body may be so large that a child gets lost in it. To offset this we may ask:

Are there chances in your school for your boy or girl to belong to smaller, more cohesive groups?

Interest groups—as drama or Spanish or debate club and so on? Hobby groups that range from TV to chess? Social groups for dances, hikes and other get-togethers? And does your school encourage boys and girls to get into High Y's, 4-H, Camp Fire groups, Scouts and the like?

Are there numerous enough and varied enough groups to provide belongingness to youngsters of all sorts?

Writes one shy adolescent:

Teen agers should get together and have parties and form clubs and have fun. In gym we should be allowed to get the boys and girls together to dance at least one day a week. That would do a lot for us.
We would be able to dance better . . .

Obviously. But more importantly:

We would get better acquainted with boys and girls we would like to meet . . .

And still more importantly:

We could learn to talk better, too, with each other.

This brings us to another facet of the peer-group matter.

Boy-girl contacts are, as we know, one of the essentials during these years. The adolescent must gradually come to form relationships that lead to knowledge of the opposite sex both as good companions and as potential good mates.

In working together in classrooms there can be exchange between the sexes which is wholesome and sound. Too often, however, this is stifled by the air of dead seriousness that pervades the scene with the little god of *study* set in a more important niche than *companionship,* which furthers the great need to *grow up.*

In classrooms there can be mutual projects. Honest laughter. The small whispered exchange of comments that build intimacy and a sense of getting to know one another.

Principal: "Don't you know you're not supposed to do that?"
Girl: "But, Miss Jones, if I let go of him, some other girl would grab him away."

Boys and girls can sit next to each other, too.

These things do not retard intellectual learning. They enhance it.

And so, here again are points to check:

In your school, has the custom of seating boys on one side of the aisle, girls on the other, been abandoned? Or when they sit in a circle for less formal discussion has the neat division been discarded in which one side of the circle is all skirts, the other all pants?

As you enter the classroom are you chilled by the still life-lessness of decorum, or are you greeted by the busy hum of healthy exchange?—A boy, for instance, leaning over a girl's desk showing her how to solve an algebra problem. Two boys and two girls around a table trying to figure out the difference on two maps of Europe drawn at two different dates.

Comes another point also in the business of peer-group relations: the matter of leadership at this age and stage.

These youngsters are turning away from the childhood years in which they have followed their parents and have been dependent on them. They now need opportunities to experience and envision themselves in more adult roles.

As the adolescent in his imagination identifies himself with his like-sexed parent, this brings with it the impetus to grow up. However, if he approaches such a role in his home, the result for him may be fraught with danger. At least in his mind.

For here once again old fantasies enter. If the boy imagines *being* Father or the girl imagines *being* Mother, the whole triangle of the earlier love-rivalry period may be brought back into play. The adolescent is then confronted once more with the earlier imagined temptation and danger of wanting to shove the like-sexed parent out. He may as a result of these fantasies grow frightened, if for no other reason than that he still needs this parent realistically as a parent, and knows that he cannot actually shoulder the responsibilities of taking his place.

This is one of the reasons why at home the teen-ager often remains more babyish, more retiring and less efficient than he needs to. He shows less independence and leadership. Or he covers up fear of being the boss by denying the fear through going to the opposite extreme and overdoing the bossing act.

In school, however, he can have opportunities for taking

[227]

bigger and more important roles realistically with less imagined danger.

Here, for example, is Bart, who has demonstrated no leadership whatsoever. He is timid and lacking in confidence and is poor in his studies. In woodshop he does his best work. This fact is brought out in a "guidance conference," where his various teachers meet to discuss his needs with the school psychologist.

As a result, his program is rearranged so that he goes into a second and less advanced shop group to assist the teacher. Here Bart helps one boy learn to run the lathe and another to square off measurements. In so doing he can identify himself in fantasy with someone bigger and more capable like the big father he admired when he was small and like his teacher now. He can be a kind of father here without the fantasied danger of losing his father by shoving him out.

To the uninitiated this might seem, for instance, that Bart is being given false hopes of getting a foreman's job when he goes out of school into industry, even though he does not seem to have foreman capabilities. This is not the important thing. Bart is learning more than anything else to be a family man, to approach adulthood feeling that he is capable of doing things for others and of taking a big man's role. He has something to give and he is getting a chance to give it. By virtue of this he is also given a chance to feel the warm LIKING FOR OTHERS which comes with giving and which forms the basis of adult and parental love.

Here then is another point to check:

In your school are there opportunities for many boys and girls to take parts in which they can identify with leadership, parenthood and giving?

For instance: Instead of officers' positions for each class as

[228]

a whole, are there group officers' positions in many small groups to spread the opportunities of holding office?

And, far more important, do these boys and girls have opportunities to show that they actually do have something to give to others? Do they have chances to recite when the teacher KNOWS THAT THEY KNOW? For this is when they have something to offer. Or does the teacher call on them only when he challenges their knowledge?

Are these boys and girls given chances to help each other individually in many areas so that they use their potentialities in anticipation of what it feels like to be a giving adult?

DOES YOUR SCHOOL PROVIDE FOR INDIVIDUAL DIFFERENCES AND DIFFERINGS?

In addition to feeling solidly *in* a group, the adolescent, as we have seen, needs to feel himself emerging from the group. Not only does he need to feel that he is LIKE OTHERS. He needs to feel that he is LIKE HIMSELF; that he *is* himself. That he has his own identity.

He needs to discover through experience that he can be himself and differ from others and yet be accepted by others. He needs to know that because of his differences and his differings, he will not be left isolated and alone.

One of the values of group support as we have sketched it is that it provides opportunities for differences and differings at the same time that it assures group belongingness. It does this for many kinds of children in many kinds of ways.

If a particular youngster is a "brain," he can pit his brain against others' brains. If he is brawn, he can pit his brawn. If he is mechanically minded, he can work with and compete with other mechanically minded youngsters. He may choose either to merge differences according to his wants and the demands of others, or he may maintain them.

[229]

He may even leave a peer group which has served as a home and find that he can survive and function comfortably and intimately in another home group of peers. This is a kind of preview for him of what it will be like later to leave his family's home and function comfortably in a home of his own, with the sound intimacy that contains of necessity differences as well as agreements.

With his peers he can voice his differences vigorously. He can stand up for what he believes one moment and retract not too long after without loss of caste. He can argue vociferously. He can debate his own cause.

These things he can do if given the opportunities. And he needs to do them not only in unsupervised moments on the playground and in the recreation hall. He needs also to do them in the classroom where a trained person can help him manage impulses which otherwise might bewilder, confuse and hold him back.

And so, here again is a point to check as a sort of indication as to whether such opportunities exist:

In your school how are classes conducted? Are there recitations only? Or are there opportunities aplenty for alive and lively *discussion*?

Must a youngster sit in obedient silence and speak only when spoken to? Must he raise his hand and then give pat answers to show only that he can say back what has been told him? Must he recite only the learned phrases that the learned ones have set?

Or—

Does the hum of interchange go on in study periods? Does the back and forth of energetic conversation prevail in his classes? Does he have chances to voice his own opinions? Does he have chances to argue his cause? Chances even to argue for the sake of argument, not alone to prove facts?

All of this brings us to a third big question in regard to a program of planfully including emotions in education:

DOES YOUR SCHOOL PROVIDE OPPORTUNITIES
FOR TALK ABOUT SELF, FOR AIRING TROUBLES
AND VOICING GRIPES?

We know well by now that troubles off the chest can become less troublesome. We know well that grievances let out through undangerous channels can offset much dangerous grief. We know that anger and hostility granted similar venting can lessen and make way for more positive feelings. We know that talking about how one feels may help feelings become less disturbing so that they can flow more freely toward constructive goals.

When inner compelling concerns come out into the open and are met with acceptance and understanding, they can lose some of their power to constrict and hold back maturing and emotional growth.

And so you might check:

Does your school do these things? Are personal feelings allowed to enter? Are they accepted? Do they become part of what is dealt with consciously in the classroom? Part of the teacher's focus?

In the last analysis PERSONAL FEELINGS lie at the core and center of "emotional education." Unless these are considered in more than haphazard fashion we do not help our young people to do what is far more important than amassing information. We do not teach them to handle themselves.

DOES YOUR SCHOOL PROVIDE CHANCES
FOR "EMOTIONAL EDUCATION" IN ITS CLASSROOMS?

Let us glimpse how this can be done!

Let us go into a few classrooms and see what a few teachers do.

Let's drop into a room marked "English and Social Studies"

Here in a high school B12 room the focus is on "problems of democracy." The boys and girls have pulled their chairs into a circle and sit comfortably, the teacher's chair in the circle also.

"It's strange," she is saying, "the way we came to be doing what we're doing. But perhaps not so strange . . ."

"No, I don't think it is," one bright-eyed girl picks up the words. "We started out talking about the American Revolution and then you asked how we would have felt if we'd been among the rebels. And then Bob made a crack about not having to imagine that far back . . ."

"No, I didn't," Bob protests. "I started to tell how *I* would have felt. And then, don't you remember? Miss Gibbs said that I was talking as if I were really feeling rebellious . . ."

"Bob's right!" from the dark wisp of a girl sitting next to him, "and then Miss Gibbs said that lots of people, in fact everybody, feels rebellious at times in their lives."

"And then we began on the things we've felt rebellious about . . ."

"And she said we could really say how we really feel, no punches pulled."

"And Jim said he didn't see what that had to do with problems of democracy. And Miss Gibbs asked us and we decided that since it's the people that make the democracy, and since *we* are the people, *our* feelings count."

"That was after Elaine wrote that poem about hatred. That poem made an impression on me. I'd like to hear it again."

"Read it again, Elaine, won't you?"

"Yes," from several. "Go on, Elaine, do."

Blushing a trifle, Elaine opened her notebook, paged the leaves and began:

I dislike the hatred
That some people have in their hearts.
That some students have
    When they laugh at another's slowness—
That some teachers have
    When they sound off on a student
    Knowing he can't sound back.

I hate the hatred that grows into wars—
Hatred that keeps the Whole World from being friends . . .

"After Elaine wrote that poem was when Miss Gibbs told
us about psychology. I think psychology's the most interesting
subject I ever heard! . . . Well, anyway, I remember how
Miss Gibbs said that Elaine's poem had 'universality'—isn't
that the word?—because all people have hate in their hearts.
You have to know you have it in yourself too, and not pretend
there's none of it there. Otherwise it piles up and then you
sometimes do something that hurts somebody you really don't
want to hurt, like your children when you have them. Or you
do something rash. That's why it's better for us to learn to do
something unrash about it . . ."

"Like writing about how you feel."

Miss Gibbs nodded. "That's how we came to be writing
about our feelings. And talking about them . . ."

"You know, Miss Gibbs," from a brown-haired girl
eagerly, "you know what makes me simply furious? My mother
goes to a parent class where some lady lectures to them.
Lectures are all right in their place! But this lady, you see,
does all the talking all the time, and my mother just sits and
listens. And if you ask me, I think psychology is right, that
you just don't learn much by sitting and listening because the
first thing you know, you don't want to listen. And then your
mind wanders off . . . Well, what I was going to tell you was
that this woman lectures on the problems of the adolescent.

But as far as my mother's concerned, absolutely none of it sinks in.

"I think what my mother and my father both need are more outlets. Someone to talk *to* about *their* feelings. Then my father wouldn't have to yell so much *at me* . . ."

"You said it, Jane. Let's face it!" from a towering boy all shoulders and muscle. "I get so furious too. My parents judge me before I have a chance to state my cause according to my constitutional rights . . ."

"Which was just how people felt at the time of the Revolution. Just like us."

"They felt they had a right to be heard . . ."

"So do we!"

Boy who is taking the role of employer, well versed psychologically: "Were you always good to your father and mother?"
Potential employee: "Of course—always."
Employer: "Sorry, my man. Then we won't want you in this plant; you'll get even with them by taking it out on us."

"But," from Elaine, thoughtfully, "since we've been heard here I don't seem to have to shout so much at my sister at home. That always got me in a spot I didn't want to be in. I'd end by getting the blame. I stand up for my rights at home just as much now. Perhaps even more. But I do it differently and I get further with it. I'm not always so ready to burst . . ."

Miss Gibbs approached the matter one way. Other teachers use other approaches—through psychodrama and sociodrama, for instance, in which feelings are played out in scenes which the young people themselves make up as they go along. Teachers do such things believing that as feelings come out into the open, boys and girls are in a better position to act in more controlled ways, albeit less timidly. For they become less afraid to be aggressive when a situation demands it. They are less fearful that their normal adolescent drive toward rebellion will flare into too great and overpowering hate.

Let's go through a door marked "Science"

The group here is talking about plant foods, with the teacher, Mr. Graham, leading the discussion.

"What foods poison plants?" asks a girl, and her teeth clamp over the knuckle of her thumb.

Mr. Graham senses tension and swiftly appraises the group. Boys and girls are leaning forward, picking at nails, biting pencils, faces lowered or thrust upward with neck muscles tight.

"Hm," thinks Mr. Graham, "there's far more emotional questioning here than in the question that's been voiced."

Aloud he says, "People are interested in poisons," reflecting the interest that has become so evident.

"Yes," short Danny explodes. "Much! Much! You tell me, Mr. Graham," his voice pleading, "please, you tell? Does drink poison *me?*"

[235]

Chairs creak. Feet shuffle. One or two giggle nervously. Then a dark boy with eyes the soft brown of moleskin volunteers, "Remember, Mr. Graham, I asked you that same question two years ago."

"Of course, Jaime. Of course I remember."

With all that had happened before and after, Mr. Graham would never forget . . .

Always on Monday mornings, the truant officer had had to go after Jaime. He'd belonged to one of the worst gangs in the area. He'd been one of the worst of the school's "bad" boys. Stealing. Destroying property. Attacking neighborhood gangs.

And then, in Mr. Graham's room, several things had occurred.

The first, he recalled, was when the class was studying the reproductive organs of frogs.

"I'd rather be a frog than a cold fish," someone had remarked.

"But a frog's still a cold-blooded animal."

"I'd rather be a rabbit."

"What? Not a person?" Mr. Graham had questioned with a responsive twinkle in his eye.

Jaime, he remembered, had looked up, astonished that feelings were being met instead of curtailed. And he'd looked more astonished, abashed and yet at the same time grateful when Mr. Graham had added, "Many boys and girls are more interested in people than in any other animal . . . It's hard at your age, though, to talk about such things in such a large mixed group. But I'm sure there are lots of important things connected with sex and birth that you'd like to talk about. I'm available, as you know, here in this room during fifth period on Tuesdays and Thursdays to talk about that or anything else if you want to come in."

[236]

Many had.

They had come individually at first. Then several boys had come together and this nucleus had grown until ten of them were meeting regularly once a week to talk about those personal and sexual problems too intimate for a larger group. A number of girls had done the same. Some of these came in individually as well.

"I believe it's essential," said Mr. Graham, *"when adolescents talk about sex in groups or have sex education of any sort offered in groups, they should also have recourse to individual conferences."*

In this Mr. Graham was exceedingly wise. Group sex education may be enough for some. It may bring much needed clarification. But with some boys and girls it may set off unconscious fantasies and anxieties which call for individual attention.

In Mr. Graham's conference period which he had twice a week, he carried the same boys and girls all through school. He remained group counselor for these particular individuals. "In this way," he said, "I have time to help them work out more of their emotional problems than if I were to have them only for one or two semesters. Because I was interested, I took special training to do such counseling. Even so, I refer a boy or girl every so often for more intensive psychological help."

In Mr. Graham's room the door stood open to Jaime as to the others. But Jaime had not come.

"He doesn't trust me enough," Mr. Graham had thought.

And then a second episode had occurred. It happened when the class was drawing the heart and circulatory system of the much-giggled-at rabbit.

Mr. Graham had been walking around the room. As he passed Jaime's seat he noticed that Jaime's drawing was not of a rabbit but of a nude woman in an indecent pose. Jaime looked up and their eyes met for an instant. And then the door opened and the principal came in with two visitors.

Swiftly Jaime flipped his paper over. He started to draw the rabbit's heart with trembling hand, his whole body huddling in terror.

Mr. Graham wondered: Did the boy expect that he would expose him?

The visitors wandered around and went out.

They had seen Jaime working on the same anatomical drawings as all the others. They did not know that on the other side of the paper lay an obscene, hidden thing.

Mr. Graham had guarded Jaime's secret. Nor did he scold him for it when the visitors had left. He granted Jaime the emotional immunity that these children must have when they expose themselves. To be neither betrayed nor condemned. For then and then only can they continue to bring out what may be preying on their minds.

When the class was over, Jaime stayed on. "Thank you, Mr. Graham," he gulped.

There was an asking look about him. And then, quite unexpectedly, the question had come. "Mr. Graham? Will drink poison *me?*"

That had been the beginning. Into Mr. Graham's counseling periods on Tuesdays and Thursdays Jaime came thereafter of his own volition. As he talked his story unfolded.

He was worried, terribly worried. Terribly frightened. The police had caught him with other boys in the gang's hide-out. They had told his family he was "bad." But this was nothing new. It merely confirmed what his family had always labeled him.

"They are going to send me, they say, to reform school. Or to a boarding school, as strict as they can find. They are going to send me away!" And there the people would surely think he was crazy because he had bad dreams at night and would wake up screaming. They would put him in an institution for the insane.

He must stay at home. His only living brother was there now. But Jaime didn't know for how long. Just till he got well enough to go back in the Army. And when he went, he might get killed like his older brother had been killed in Korea.

And pretty soon, Jaime too would be old enough to go into the Army and he also might get hurt or killed.

What was a person to do? Only one other person besides this brother had ever loved him. The brother who'd died! His mother never had. Nor his father either. "They're always too busy quarreling. Too busy with their own troubles."

Could he get relief in drink? Relief in sex? Could he find some girl friend and take her with him and run away? He'd wanted to, but no girl really liked him.

Every week end he'd been drinking to forget.

And so every Monday morning he'd been "sick" and "poisoned" and had been truant from school.

Two years had passed since then. Very gradually, things had grown better. Several Sunday nights Mr. Graham had used the address of a new hide-out furtively given him with Jaime's plea that he come there and get him home so he could be sober before Monday morning. Then he'd put Jaime on his own. And Jaime had responded to the trust put in him.

No longer were there Monday truancies. Moreover, during the past summer Jaime had been a hundred per cent reliable on the job he'd held packing groceries in a market.

Now, in the classroom, it was Jaime who gave the answer to the other boy's question whether drink would poison. It hung in the tense air, this other boy's question: "Does drink poison *me?*"

"Drink . . ." says Jaime, thoughtful and sober. "When you

drink too much you've got poison already in your mind. Most likely you drink to think you feel better. Only afterward it makes you remember worse . . ."

They talked seriously of drinking and its effects and of what some of these boys and girls had seen of drunkenness and of their own fears in connection with it. And gradually the discussion moved away from fear to more deliberative thinking. "My folks are French. In France people think you're strange if you drink water instead of wine with your meals. So we have a carafe on our table always, and we drink wine for water. It's always been that way in our home."

"In our home my folks have cocktails when they have company. When I was young I used to have a Coke when they had cocktails. Now that I'm older I have some sherry."

"My family never drinks. They don't believe in it."

"In some homes you drink; in some you don't," Mr. Graham summarizes the particular point under focus. "Whether it's permitted or not depends on your particular parents' judgments and beliefs . . . Drinking outside the home involves other problems . . ."

"My parents forbid it."

"Even a beer?"

"It's against the law in public places when you're under age."

"And it gets you so 'high' you forget what you're supposed to remember."

"And it's certainly dangerous when you're driving a car."

"It would be a relief to know I could drink at home some without my parents' landing hard on me. I think then I wouldn't have to drink so much . . ."

"You mean you drink to fight them?"

"That's a thought."

Different customs.

Different propulsions.

Different feelings.

A far cry from sticking to textbooks. "But why should you?" asks Mr. Graham. "It's easier to get through the textbooks after some of the pressures have been relieved. My boys and girls come back to the printed page, concentrate better and cover material far more rapidly after I've gone with them up those side roads and byroads to explore what they feel."

Let's see what happens in "Art"

"When I think what I used to do and how I used to teach, it makes me sad," exclaims Mrs. Collins. "I used to think perpetually of the ground that needed to be covered and the art problems that needed to be tackled instead of the human problems. Now I think of both.

"I don't know just exactly when I changed. But I do remember one day several years ago, I was walking through the room quietly looking at the charcoal still lifes the youngsters were working on, when I came upon one boy who was doodling on some scratch paper. He didn't notice me for a few moments. And when he did, he hurriedly shoved the scratch-pad sheet under his drawing board.

" 'What were you doing, John?' I asked.

"Perhaps because he caught my interest and curiosity and could see that I wasn't feeling like an avenging angel, he pulled the sheet back into view without protest.

"What he'd done was to draw those penmanship whorls very big at the edge and going down into swirling blackness as the circles decreased in size. And then I noticed a figure, contorted, as if whirling down through the cone.

"Something about the thing gripped me and I think he must have felt this because he said, 'It's a vortex,' very simply. Then he added, 'And the figure's *me.*'

"Meanwhile two or three others had come over to see.

[241]

" 'You feel that way sometimes!' I said, remembering back to my own adolescence.

"I noticed others nodding. 'I do, and it's awful,' Sally confided. 'You feel so confused sometimes . . .' And several others chimed in.

"That's how we started drawing HOW-I-FEEL pictures in that group.

"In subsequent groups I've opened the possibilities by saying that people their age have a great many different sorts of feelings. At times they feel confused, at times hilarious. At times very low. At times as if the world were against them. At times as if they hated certain people terribly much.

"And I've said they could draw or sketch or paint how they feel. Or what they'd like to do when they feel a certain way . . .

"When I opened it up in one group, for instance, a lot of them wanted to drown, burn, bury the attendance officer. Many were angry at teachers who regimented them and took 'liberty away.'

" 'This is Mr. X. The ugliest man in the world. I hate him.' His teeth in the primitive drawing were black. His face was scarred. His body was grotesquely proportioned and bent.

" 'Mr. X?' Several tittered with the surge of kindred feelings.

" 'Guess who Mr. X is?' Jeremy cajoled the others.

" 'I think he's the policeman who arested me yesterday for leaving the car parked too long,' from a lanky girl.

" 'He's my uncle,' from a boy who had no father. 'He comes over all the time and criticizes my mother for being too easy on me.'

" 'He's the exact replica of my dad when he gets angry . . .'

" 'He's like the way I feel when I get mad.'

"No particularly deep or dark feelings were brought out among them . . ." Mrs. Collins explains. "But it served as a starter. The youngsters caught onto the fact that angry feelings are natural and are better gotten off the chest.

"As one boy put it, 'It's better to show in a picture that you're mad than it is to throw rocks through windows in the kind of riots some kids stage.' "

So it is.

"Often," says Mrs. Collins, "they draw feelings without realizing it at first. I've come to see that when the girls do fashion designs they are often thinly veiling their own yearnings for better figures, for glamorous looks. And so, instead of focusing on impersonal problems, we're tying this subject in with more personal wishes. 'Clothes I'd like to have.' . . . 'How I'd like to look.' "

Many times, Mrs. Collins tells us, when boys and girls are given chances to draw about feelings, their academic work improves. "And as for the techniques they need in art, they get these. There are times we dig into purely technical problems of drawing or of color. Sometimes we get at them in relation to their FEELING pictures. But they don't have to monopolize the scene."

With clay, too, many things can happen. Not the least of them the return-to-messing activities that many an adolescent manifests in the messing his parents have to contend with at home.

"Iggh!" crows dainty, fussy petite Diane, who her mother claims is "the world's filthiest child about the house."

"Iggh! I love the feel of it. Just slishing it. Please, Mrs. Collins, let me slish awhile. Don't make me get to work making something right away."

*Let's take a very brief glimpse
into a "Homemaking" room*

Says Greta, "I love to sew!"

Proudly she spreads the sheet she has made. The right size

for a crib for the baby brother or sister she is expecting.

"I've got to choose a design to embroider that will be suitable for either a girl or a boy."

"When I have a baby," says Peggy, "I'm going to have every-

Nursery-schooler, violently banging the clay, is chanting a chant of his own making:

"Rockabye
Rockabye
Baby! Baby!
Sockabye
Sock my baby sister!
Sockabye; sock her hard."

High-school member of Family Life Class, to himself: "Gee! That sure makes me see how I felt when I was little. I never realized it before."

thing pink. I don't care what sex the baby is. I like pink and I don't see why you have to stick to convention."

"When I have a baby I'm not going to bring it up conventionally. Or at least not the way I was brought up. So strictly you couldn't have any fun."

"What do you mean, Stell?" Mrs. Royce wonders.

With this they are off. Into things that they've felt about

their own upbringing, airing old grievances, saying what they didn't like and what they did like; what made them sad, what made them happy.

And from there they set out into dreams of growing up and having families of their own.

Where these girls—and boys, too—have opportunities to observe in nursery schools, many important associations to their own younger days arise naturally.

However, to get back to Mrs. Royce. Again the things her girls are making are not the main issue. They are well made, it is true, and Mrs. Royce has given help aplenty on technical skills. But her major concern is not on *things*. It's on *people*. This leads us to the major question you will want to check in your school:

Does your school
have TEACHERS WHO ARE INTERESTED
not only in what they teach
but also in
THE PEOPLE WHOM THEY TEACH?

IN YOUR SCHOOL IS THERE GUIDANCE THAT COUNTS?

For many years, guidance was the domain of a school psychologist or counselor. It consisted mainly in arranging programs, or attending to college applications, or administering tests and in giving advice if a pupil's grades went down.

Fortunately now the concept of guidance is expanding. We are realizing that guidance in a school must go much further. What guidance actually adds up to is *emotional education*. As such it cannot be done by just one person. It must be included in the classroom, as we have described, and in many additional ways.

The school psychologist can act as a coordinator and as a resource person. His job should not be restricted to lifeless matters. Because it has to do with the core of life itself for

[245]

these teen-agers, it must also spread to the lives of those who deal with them. It must spread to include teachers and parents. In short, if it is to count: GUIDANCE SHOULD TAKE CHILDREN, PARENTS AND TEACHERS INTO ACCOUNT.

One of the problems of the school psychologist is to see that a youngster gets one teacher like Mr. Graham or Mrs. Collins or Miss Gibbs. A teacher who serves his group as counselor as well as teacher.

In this way, a teacher like Mr. Graham can stand as a school parent to a boy like Jaime. Since Mr. Graham had classes with Jaime all through the grades at this school, Jaime could deepen his contacts with him. He didn't have to uproot confidence before it had time to become firmly embedded. His trust could grow in a way that would have been practically impossible if Jaime had needed to change his group counselor from one semester to the next.

Moreover, it was only in Mr. Graham's room that intimate talk went on with Jaime and his particular group. Other teachers had their particular *counseling groups*.

Had Jaime failed to get along comfortably with Mr. Graham, his group counselor might have been changed.

From time to time the psychologist discussed Jaime's difficulties with Mr. Graham. At times he called conferences with all Jaime's teachers in order to work out the best possible opportunities for Jaime in the school. He also talked with Mr. Graham about seeing Jaime's parents and working with them.

Obviously not all teachers are able to include emotional education in their work with children. Teachers are people. They too have been brought up to be afraid of feelings—of their own in particular. And far too frequently, basic attention to children's emotions has been left out of their teacher training.

This points to another need which you will want to consider: In their professional training all teachers need experiences which will help them learn about children's feelings, children's fantasies, children's real and imagined reactions to their families. They also need experiences that will help them understand more about themselves and their own feelings.

In their professional training all teachers should have chances to work with young children in nursery schools. For many adolescent problems hark back to the nursery years. In their professional training, teachers should learn from child therapists how children's imaginations function, and how natural and universal to childhood are many seemingly bizarre and strange feelings and thoughts.

As for themselves and their own feelings, as they work with children under sensitively attuned guidance, teachers should be helped to let the impact of observing how these children feel relate to their own feelings, both present and past. They should have chances to think and talk about themselves and how they felt in their own adolescence and earlier. They can do this both individually and in small, intimate groups, just as the youngsters did in their groups with Mr. Graham. Such experiences should be part of the teachers' regular professional training so that the understanding and acceptance of their own feelings enables them to become more acceptant and understanding of the adolescent's. But, as we have said, this sort of thing has seldom happened in the days when these, our teachers, were originally trained! Again, however, it isn't too late! Given the wish, the will and the flexibility on their part, and the right sort of teacher of teachers to guide them, they still can learn.

So, once more, here is something of the utmost importance in your schools:

What about your teachers' education for educating? Has *it* included emotional education? If not, how can you see that at least some of your teachers have such educational opportunities provided them now?

If the school psychologist has had the proper training himself, he can make himself available to individual teachers who may explore with him what they need in terms of their own emotional education. He can tell them where they can get it. He can also, if he himself has had the proper preparation, help them to deepen their understandings by the discussions he has with them singly and in groups. (If the school psychologist lacks this training, outside resources can be called in.)

There can be groups also with parents. Groups to think more deeply on the needs of adolescence. To think more squarely about how parents feel as parents and as people. Groups to give parents as well as children the emotional support and increasing awareness which parents, in these days of crisis, seek and need.

THIS THEN IS YOUR SCHOOL

What the schools might do if they considered the emotions more deeply holds untold possibilities.

Should you find your schools lacking, the matter does not have to rest there. You can form parents' groups or citizens' groups to bring *emotional education* into the place it should have.

In this direction lies a tremendous dream for the future. A dream which we need desperately to convert into reality. A dream of home and school working together to give to the generations who shall inherit the earth an inner awareness of their own emotions so that they may translate this in turn into an awareness of others. Themselves more knowingly aware of the needs of human beings—equipped with the only awareness that can ever produce a decent world.

[248]

15. With Firmer Step

During all the long years of our children's growing, we have doubtless both feared and looked forward to the day when we would be able to say, "Here stand these young and hopeful people, facing their own futures, firm on their own feet."

Before these children of ours reach manhood and womanhood, however, they must take steps which are often difficult for us to endure.

We need to stand by, for one thing, and watch them gradually come to accept their masculinity or femininity and to grant it honor. To know themselves male or female. To feel that they can function in their own sex roles in life and not have to proclaim it artificially by masculine blustering or feminine fluttering.

We need to see them developing their own intimacies outside our family's orbit in relationships that become more intimate and more essential to them than their relationship with us.

We need to watch them find their own economic place in the world and know their own worth as adults realistically facing the problems of earning a living.

And we need to see them grow apart from us and go on their own way in their own right, with their own personal orientation, integration and integrity. With their own unique selfhood.

The achievement of these goals by our children has its desirable side for us as persons in our own right. It has its undesirable side as well. "When I think of my children grown up, I feel as if I had two faces. One bright and smiling. The other sad at the loss of them and apprehensive in wondering: What now about me?"

So many years of our lives have been spent as parents. So much thought and emotional energy has been invested in bringing up our children. We look forward to the task accomplished. But we also feel somewhat fearful that the days ahead may be empty and bleak.

And so the last lap of helping our children to grow up is fraught with conflict for us, their parents. It calls for wisdom and forbearance and fortitude in us. And for thought focused on ourselves as well as on them.

HEADS IN THE CLOUDS; FEET ON THE GROUND

As the adolescent progresses, the flying-high and the settling-down parts of him are both in evidence. He is apt to be an idealist and a philosopher. Cynical sometimes. But his cynicism on the whole is shot through with the bright threads of faith that he will do his bit in creating a new and better world.

What should be done about international policies. About minorities. About graft and politics. Legal reforms. Prostitution. How the mysteries of life and death and immortality might be solved.

His certainties in these matters may help offset his uncertainty in more practical affairs—on jobs, for instance. For it takes time to settle on the kind of work he wants to do. He is apt to change several times before he finds the vocation of his choice just as he changes also in finding the mate of his choice. We need to encourage but not push.

"I've got to get a job." . . . "I want to go to college." . . .

"How can it be managed?" . . . "Will I need to combine the two?"

As he gathers more certainty, some of his ideas will mesh with ours. Others will depart more vigorously from our ideas for him and move on their own separate way.

Says Stan's father, "We want you to continue college."

"But I don't want to, Dad. I've thought it all over. Very carefully. The two years of junior college have been fine. But I want to go to work now. I want to earn more money than I can on a part-time plan."

"Well, Stan," thoughtfully, "I won't say I'm not disappointed. I am, and your mother will be too. We'll still try to persuade you. We'll give you our views. We'll give you our reasons. And we won't try to hide what our feelings are. But whatever you finally decide, we'll stand behind you. That you know well."

"You bet I do, Dad. And I'm terribly grateful. I'd hate it if you were like Tom's folks. His mother flew into a rage, then had weeks of hysterics and now goes around moaning and groaning that Tom is killing her, breaking her heart. And his father says he'll disown him if Tom doesn't stay in school."

Ned and his father have other differences.

"I've looked forward all my life, Ned, to having you come into the store with me."

"But, Father, hardware's not my line. I've had good luck raising chickens for years, ever since that first setting hen you gave me when I was ten. I want to go into the business now on a larger scale. I talked to Mr. Brown at the bank about financing, and I've got it all set."

Here is a lawyer whose young son wants to be a musician and has what it takes. Here is an engineer whose son is interested in the grocery business and doesn't want to study to become a partner in his father's firm.

Here is a girl whose family has had high social ambitions

for her, but what she wants to do is to go on with biochemical research.

Nor is it only in terms of ambition that our children may differ. Their codes and ideals may depart from ours. We may not smoke or drink. They do. We may not be churchgoers. They are. We may be sticklers for etiquette while they decide to travel the Bohemian path.

All these things, and many others like them, we can take as insults. We can consider them evidence that we, as parents, have fallen short.

"He's thrown over the very things we've labored and slaved to give him. Now he's turning us down. This proves he doesn't love us."

Quite naturally if he goes counter to our wishes and ambitions for him, we shall be disappointed. Angry, too, maybe, at least for a while.

But neither his "contrary" actions nor our unhappy feelings are at all true indications that we've failed as parents. His opposition does not at all disprove his love.

Actually, a young person may follow his parents' dictates and love them far less than he would have loved them had he broken away. His outside compliance may cover an inner revolt far greater because it is pent up.

Remember: He is an individual. As an individual he may choose to go opposite to us. Finding that he can go opposite may be his surest road to finding also that he loves us well. For love flourishes best without shackles that bind.

Differences in his way of life from our way of life do not mean that we have failed. We cannot expect him to agree always with us. Differences are only natural. When a child of ours goes on *his* way, whether or not this is *our* way does not matter. If he goes steadily, following his own thoughtful direction, holding his head high, feeling assured and confident in being himself—this is a sign that our job's been well done.

"Mother," Beth asks, "do you remember my various boy friends? Larry was the first one, if you'll recall. We'd walk to school together and I thought it was swell to have a boy pay me attention. But the drip didn't even offer to carry my books.

"And then there was Arthur. We'd go to the park, sit on the bench, and gaze at the moon by the hour. He'd hold my hand. Did I get a thrill! I felt so wild and demonish and grown-up. But when I sort of hinted around for him to kiss me, he got preacherish and told me he had ideals.

"That threw me into wild-man Jack's arms. Boy, was he fast! He had that hot rod. And I had ten fits making him turn his muffler off so you and Dad wouldn't tell me I couldn't go out with such a monster. And boy, how he would try to neck. I didn't have to do any inviting. In fact, I had to fight him off, and I thought that was terrific. It made me feel so sophisticated. And as if I really rated. But when he suggested that we run off and take a freighter to South America, I called it quits.

"Then there was Marty, and Ben, and Nick and Ted . . . What a bunch! All of them nice, though, in their own ways. But none as tops as Hal. I thought each was the one. But Hal is different. Or I'm different. Maybe that's it. Anyway, I feel easy with him. Really easy. Even though I don't intend to make a practice of it, I wouldn't care if he saw me in curlers or with cream on my face. I wouldn't care if he heard me in my vilest humor. Neither of us has to be consistently on our best behavior. He takes me as me, and I take him as him. It's so much better that way."

As Beth and Hal went through their engagement period and into their marriage, their relationship deepened. They liked to work and play and be together. There was a fullness and roundness to their intimacy. It was solid and good. Theirs was a willingness to share. A mutual trust. Thoughtfulness for each other in love and in sex. A willingness too to bring differences into the open and an ability to get anger and aggravations out and over with, and to restore "the lines of closer communication," as Beth phrased it.

"They've got something sound in their marriage," Muriel, Beth's mother, mused a bit ruefully. "They're so complete with each other that I just don't count. I know I shouldn't be so eager to. But with my only chick gone, I feel . . . well, empty. On one hand I'm glad she's happy. On the other I feel lost.

"The lack reaches into Paul's life with me also. I hadn't realized how much of our time together was spent on Beth. We had become 'Father and Mother,' and had neglected being 'husband and wife'! We'd lost touch with ourselves, too, as well as with each other. I can see that we've got a lot to get back."

So they consciously set about developing new, middle-aged interests. "Togetherness" was one good, sound aim.

"We've taken to reading aloud! And we're following the exhibits at the county museum. We're going to more shows, too. And doing more entertaining, picking up with old friends and gathering new ones . . ."

And since Muriel did not have a business, as Paul did, to occupy her, she started to develop new interests of her own. With her natural bent for outgoing sociability, she went into the hospitality committee in her church, and into the thrift shop of a local charitable organization.

She did not sit around as did Rita's mother and moan dejectedly, "My daughter's growing old and I'm growing older. She'll generate while I degenerate. It's no fun!"

There's no need for any of us to degenerate.

When our boy or girl learns to be more richly himself in himself and with others, and most particularly with another person of his own generation, we too can become more richly ourselves.

[254]

Life has not passed us by because our children are no longer dependent on us. We, as well as they, have our own good life to live.

In our children's children we shall find regeneration. But to *depend* and lean on them to give us sustenance for ourselves —this makes us a burden instead of a help.

Just as Paul and Muriel found activities suited to their bents and interests, so have other men and women found other activities.

"There's so much to do. And so much that needs doing!"

"I'm in things up to my neck. But that's better by far than sitting around waiting for my sons and daughters to telephone to me, and feeling hurt when they don't."

Many women find their main interest remaining where it has rested for so many years.

"What I know and love best are children! They've been my whole life!"

All right. Let them remain so. Only spread out your arms. There are so many children in so many situations who need your attention and care!

Can you volunteer to work in some child-care agency? In some church group? On some board? How about forming a committee to look into what your local schools are doing about educating children's emotions as well as their minds?

It occurred to one group of women whose children were married to form a grandmother's branch of their PTA. It occurred to a second group to form a grandmother's auxiliary of a cooperative nursery school; to a third to help with school transportation.

Ask yourself:

What are my interests?

What can I do and what would I like to do so that life may remain full of healthy demands?

What have I always promised myself I'd get into, given the opportunity and the necessary time?

IN SPITE OF MISTAKES

All our lives, of course, our children remain our children to us in our hearts. Even so, their lives are not our lives. We shall cherish their successes. We shall grieve over their failures.

Happy Day!

We shall be glad in their joys and unhappy in the face of their problems and sorrows. And sometimes we shall find ourselves blaming ourselves for whatever ills befall them. "If only I hadn't made such mistakes!"

This too is natural. But to dwell on it and stop there is unproductive.

We've all made mistakes. They're done. We cannot undo them. Blaming ourselves for them is futile. We do better as we acknowledge that making mistakes has been as much a part of living as life itself.

We, as well as our children, have had times of fear and uncertainty; of hate and of anger. We still shall have them. They are bound to come as long as we live.

Where are we now?

[256]

What of the future?

Isn't there some word we can carry with us to hold close and live by as time moves on?

There is. This is it:

We have come through the long years, often without knowing that feelings are as important as we now know they are.

This new awareness can help us bring greater richness to live by than anything else. It can help us help others. It can enable us to reach out beyond ourselves and beyond our own families into new kinds of giving.

We have learned to acknowledge the importance of our children's feelings and of our own. We have gained in ACCEPTANCE and UNDERSTANDING of feelings within our own family circle.

Outside our family circle there are countless people hungry for acceptance, understanding and love.

These are valuable gifts to be given. They are also great and universal tools. With them we can build stronger bridges across the spaces that separate man from man.

We no longer need to struggle and push to attain perfection or to have our children and our children's children attain it.

We can stand firm and proud and unashamed in the frailty and strength of admitting: Yes, I am human like all the earth's people. Yet I am capable of a great and good and growing capacity to accept, to love and to understand.

Index

Emotional needs, 22–23, 75–76

Fact and fiction, in adolescent problems, 36–47
in early sex education, 99–102
Facts of life, teen-ager's own, with clear details, 87–93, 95
Fantasies, early, understanding of, in sex education, 99–102, 109–118
effect of, on behavior, 6–8
importance of, in shaping attitudes, 39
about separation and divorce, 205–209, 211–212
Fears, and fallacies in sex education, 101–102, 109–117
healing of, 127–129
of parents, 4–5
in child's feelings, 64–65
Feelings, in boy-girl contacts, 139–166, 225
of parents, when children are grown, 254–257
honesty in, 11–17
importance of, 10–21
in own adolescence, 17–19
in separation and divorce, sharing of, 210–214
understanding of, 9
personal, in schools, 221–248
in remarriage, 216–218
of teen-ager, attempts to hide, 40–47
by denying, 42–43
by disguising (see Disguises)
by running back, 40–41
bringing out, 52–55, 62–63, 65–66
through action, 69

[260]

Feelings, of teen-agers, bringing out, action planning in, 71–74
through games, 70
reducing pressure inside by, 58–62
by remembering bygones, 77–80
through spoken word, 69, 70
through written word, 69
consideration of, in matters of sex, 95
disregarding, 51
importance of, 5–8
importance of understanding, 48–82, 257
separating of, from acts, 54–57
in separation and divorce, sharing of, 214–215
unconscious, coming out of, 47–48
understanding of, 9
Firmness, necessity of, 10
Freedom for children, 10
Friends, choice of, 179–187

Guidance in schools, 245–248

Homosexuality, 154–157
latent, 156
Honesty in feelings of parents, 11–17
Hostility, 65
Household chores, payment for, 177–179
responsibilities in, 169–174
use of creative urge in, 174–177

Ideas, mistaken, effect of, on behavior, 6–8

About the Author

All her life Dorothy Baruch has been concerned with the problems of adults and young people—and has been trying to do something about them. After attending Bryn Mawr and the University of Southern California, she was graduated from Broadoaks School of Education of Whittier College at Pasadena, where some time later she was Professor of Education for several years. At Broadoaks she organized the preschool groups of which she was director. She has had experience with parent education in Los Angeles and with preschools at several other places in California.

In the meantime Dr. Baruch married and had two children of her own. As a leading consulting psychologist, she is at present doing individual and group psychotherapy with both adults and children of all ages. Dr. Baruch is author of a number of books for parents, among them NEW WAYS IN DISCIPLINE and ONE LITTLE BOY; several books for children; and many popular magazine articles and professional research reports.